The New York City Revival of 1858 And Its Lessons

A Collection of Fugitive Papers, Having Reference to the Great Awakening

By James W. Alexander

AUDUBON PRESS
2601 Audubon Drive
P.O. Box 8055
Laurel, MS 39441-8000 USA

Orders: 800-405-3788
Inquiries: 601-649-8572
Voice: 601-649-8570 / Fax: 601-649-8571
E-mail: buybooks@audubonpress.com
Web Page: www.audubonpress.com

Printed in the United States
Cover design by Crisp Graphics

ISBN # 978-09652883-9-2

Original Publication:
New York:
ANSON D. F. RANDOLPH, 683 BROADWAY
1859

Original Publication Layout and Typography:
JOHN A. GRAY, STEREOTYPER,
16 & 19 Jocob Street, N.Y.

CONTENTS

PREFACE

The short papers here for the first time gathered, had a certain measure of acceptance, less from their own merit, than from their having been struck off during the prevalence of an unusual interest in divine things. For the most part they were penned in the intervals of a hurried life, with the hope that scriptural instruction of the simplest kind might gain a hearing, at a time when every one's attention was drawn to the work of God in the land.

The occasion may be fitly seized for a brief retrospect of the scenes through which we have been led, and which, to a certain extent, surround us still; for we would fain speak of this Revival of Religion, not as past, but as present.

The greatest commercial alarm which our country ever experienced took place in the summer and autumn of the year 1857. It is unnecessary to rehearse what is imprinted on the hearts of thousands, or to open wounds which are still bleeding. Besides the great numbers who were utterly ruined, there were ten times as many whose earthly destinies seemed to be in libration. If we were to look no further than to the wear and tear of mind and brain, caused by pecuniary apprehensions and troubles in business, such as drove some to despair and madness, the evil could not be reckoned at the rate of millions of gold and silver. The writer returned to his native country after a short absence, to find as it were a pall of mourning over every house. Visitations of this kind — the remark is common concerning pestilence — often produce a hardening effect. In the present instance, it pleased God, in his marvelous loving-kindness, by the ploughshare of his judgments to furrow the ground for precious seed of salvation, and to make distresses touching worldly estate to awaken desire for durable riches and righteousness. Out of the eater came forth meat and out of the strong came forth sweetness. From the very heart of these trials emerged spiritual yearnings, thirstings, and supplications after the fountain of living waters. We can not always trace the sequence of events, but it is certain that the meetings for prayer, which noted the dawn of this great Revival, had their beginning while we were still amidst the throes of our commercial distress.

It is believed that the first of those daily prayer-meetings which have now become general, was held on the twenty-third day of September, in the year just named. The place thus honored was the Consistory-room of the North Dutch Church at the corner of William and Fulton streets. The simple pious thought of JEREMIAH LAMPHIER, and a few like-minded servants of God, was to gather a handful of business men, at the hour of noon, to confer, to read the Word, to sing, and to cry unto God for the outpouring of his Holy Spirit. But Revival was already begun. God had already poured out the Spirit of grace and of supplications. We doubt not there was a simultaneous effusion, on other groups and in other places. Prayers long treasured up were beginning to receive copious answer; prayers, of which some, we have thought, may have been offered by those venerable ministers of Holland, whose portraitures still adorn the walls of the Consistory-room. It has been questioned who first conceived the project of these meetings. The problem is unprofitable; human plans looked forward to no such results; let God have the glory!

It is not the place for a history, nor shall any thing of

the kind be now attempted.[1] Suffice it to say, this meeting so grew in numbers and interest as to demand increase of accommodation. Daily prayer meetings had not been altogether unknown, during periods of unusual awakening; but here was a large congregation of worshippers, almost all men of business, near the very centre of trade, day after day, and — as the event has proved — without abatement for a twelve-month. The great attraction was Prayer. The great business was intercession. This, as springing from the "love of the Spirit" seems especially pleasing to God, who answers us more signally when we seek the good of others. As the meeting went on, solicitude for the conversion of sinners unto God became more apparent. Requests bearing this character were greatly multiplied. From curiosity, from inward anguish, from vague alarm, from the mingled motives in which religious concern has its beginnings, numbers of worldly visitors entered the doors. Conversion after conversion was reported. Men who had felt the emptiness of earthly things, and smarted under losses, came hither for consolation. Ministers of the Gospel often embraced the opportunity to address the words of truth to assemblies singularly prepared to drink in every syllable. Other similar prayer-meetings were established in New York, of which some are continued till this day. During a brief period, Burton's Theatre, opposite to the City Hall, and capable of holding three thousand persons, was converted into a place of prayer, and was crowded. Other cities and towns speedily entered into the same labor of love, until the daily prayer-meetings of the land might be numbered by hundreds. The longest continuance of devotional interest, in immense assemblies for prayer, has probably been witnessed in the city of Philadelphia. There also has been seen the phenomenon of a widely-spread awakening among the Firemen, so that the houses occupied by their engines and associations have not unfrequently resounded with the voice of prayer and praise. The attention of the churches of Christ throughout the land was naturally attracted to the spectacle of thousands, including the busiest and hitherto the most worldly, flocking to the most unadorned exercises of devotion. It ought not to be withheld that many of these services are maintained without diminution of vigor to the moment of this writing. Meanwhile churches of every religious denomination received remarkable increase. The statistics of conversion are sometimes unsafe; where there is so much room for mistake and exaggeration, it may be wisest to venture no figures. "The Lord thy God add unto his people, how many soever they be, an hundred fold!" The report of this gracious visitation has gone abroad to other Lands, where true Christians have been led to inquire with avidity into the origin, nature, and sequel of a reformation so unprecedented.

The Church of Christ, and our American portion of it, can not be unmindful of frequent refreshings in former days. Each of these, if the means of studying them were at hand, would doubtless be found to have peculiarities of its own; arising from acknowledged diversities in the sovereign dispensation of the Spirit. The present revival of religion has some characteristics, which ought not to escape our observation.

The work of grace, in which we rejoice, was not the result of any human project, concerted arrangement, or prescribed plan. It was not an excitement foreseen, predicted, and made to order. So far from this, it stands out among kindred reformations, as differing from them all. No man pretends to have ever seen the like. And this it is of the greatest importance to record, for the silence of such as stigmatize the entire proceedings as the creations of ingenious artifice working upon overheated fancy.

Equally incontestable is it, that this great interest in things divine and eternal, did not "come with observation." There had been no pomp of preparation. Indeed the foregoing season was one of remarkable aridity and dearth; so that multitudes of the younger professing Christians had never seen what is called a Revival. And even when the holy elevation of feeling was at its height, it was, in the circle open to our survey, entirely free, on one hand, from the machinery of religious maneuver, and, on the other hand, from manifestations of an unruly enthusiasm. An exception here and there, out of thousands, lamented, suppressed, and never propagating itself, in no degree impairs the force of the assertion just made. Decorous stillness, reverent waiting upon God, and a tender sense of the heavenly presence, have marked many of these delightful assemblages.

Very striking is the truth, that this was an awakening of graces, primarily among the people of God. In this view it is most properly denominated a Revival. The influence began in the heart of the Church. Even after conversions were greatly multiplied, this characteristic was prominent. The daily meeting was of disciples. Those who came together were in the first instance, believers. Experienced pastors have observed that in the progress of this work of grace. Christians of long standing have had the inward growth remarkably quickened, have renewed their first exercises, reconsidered their evidences, ascertained the foundation under them, and attained to new sorrows and new joys.

It was, eminently, a revival of Prayer. Desires to approach God, jointly, in importunate supplication, were awakened. This was perhaps the leading characteristic. It was repeatedly noticed, that assemblies were more interested in the prayers than the addresses. They came together, not to hear learned, elegant, or eloquent appeals, but to unite in prayer. Even addresses to impenitent sinners, though often inter- mingled, did not constitute the business in hand; it was prayer. Never was this so strikingly the case. Never have we known such honor conferred upon God's ordinance of prayer. And the mode of prayer which prevailed, as has already been hinted, was Intercession. Every relation of life has appeared in tender, touching request. The applications for such intercessory address have been numberless; and if not always seasonable or judicious, they have generally been affecting. They have been transmitted hundreds of miles, and from all parts of the land.

Perhaps no fact, among all those by which this revival manifested itself, is more encouraging than that Christians of different names were in visible union. That fraternity which had been sought with less success by separate means, was here seen to flow naturally from concert in prayer, under the influences of the Holy Spirit; thus indicating it may be the source from which we are to expect the sublime unity of a coming day. Except where some unscriptural and exclusive pretensions have been trampled on, it has not been heard that any branch of the Christian Church has uttered complaint. There has been no compromise of tenets, except as to the utterance of disputed points upon the common ground. In our country at least there has never been so open an acknowledgment of varying Christians by one another; it is indeed second only to that joint participation at the Lord's' Table, which bigotry still resists, but which is the true and appointed sign of the Communion of Saints.

From the beginning of these gracious communications, ministers of the Gospel have cheerfully stood by and seen the principal share of labor in the hands of their lay brethren. The meetings for prayer were instituted, and to a great extent have been conducted, by laymen. It can never be alleged that this has been an enthusiasm stirred up by the clergy. That feelings of jealousy should ever arise between the two classes of laborers, is earnestly to be deprecated. Among any leading minds, we rejoice to believe that it does not exist.

The observation has been often made, and with the greatest truth, that among the instruments of this awakening no prominence has been given to particular men, or distinguished gifts of learning and eloquence. It is true, the stated ministrations of the sanctuary have gone on as heretofore, perhaps with less increase of preaching than has sometimes been known; diversities existing however even on this point;. But there has not been the slightest tendency, so far as appears, to magnify any special human agency, or to lean upon what is often alleged to be the inordinate strength of public exhortation. This is stated in the way of simple narration, without comment or inference.

In connection with preachers and preaching, it is proper to add, that the present revival of religion has been singularly exempt from what may be called a dogmatical aspect, and especially from a controversial spirit in regard to doctrine. Seasons of religious excitement have been known to us, in which great stress has been laid on certain tenets, as well the false as the true; and in which these have even been regarded as inseparable from the gracious influence. Nothing of the kind has been whispered in the late period of serious inquiry. Doctrines, as held by believers of different persuasions, have been set forth and inculcated in preaching and catechising, but not we believe in the spirit of the Shibboleth.

Two great truths have been made exceedingly prominent, in every stage of the revival; the influence of the Holy

Spirit, and free salvation through the righteousness of the Lord Jesus Christ. The former of these has been recognized by every act of prayer, in those meetings which chiefly revealed the general interest of Christian people. The other has stood forth in vivid illumination, in all addresses to convinced souls. If any one formula, above all others, can be said to convey the spirit of the teaching which has prevailed, it is this: COME to CHRIST. And it is a fact worthy of note, that no single publication has had wider currency than Mr. Newman Hall's "Come to Jesus."

When we consider how extensively the hearts of professing Christians have been moved, in every part pf the country; how densely the volume of prayer has gone from this body of saints; how in many of them there has been a renewal and deepening of experience, by the opening of hidden fountains within them; we can not resist the persuasion that all this great work is after all one of preparation. The Lord appears to be preparing his armaments and marshaling his hosts for new conquests. Instead, therefore, of sitting down, as if the season of blessing had come to an end, it would be more consonant with the divine dealings, if we should regard it as only begun. The summons is unquestionably to renewed faith, intercession, and labor.

The rumor of what God has done for us has gone into other lands, and believers there have inquired with eagerness into the state of the facts, the means which have been used, and the likelihood of benefit from adapting our means to their condition. Our brethren abroad have probably been prone to ascribe to our churches an absolute advancement in piety much beyond the truth. The principle should never be forgotten, that while the great laws of the divine government and the dispensation of grace remain the same, the Supreme Giver varies his modes of bounty, with reference to differences of country and period. Apostolic awakenings were in some things unlike those of the Reformation day. The quiet, spring-like renewal of vital godliness, under Spener, Francke, and the Pietists, bore little external resemblance to the prodigious revolution under the Wesleys, Whitefield, Edwards, the Tennents and the Blairs. The very remarkable awakenings in which Dr. Nettleton and his friends were instrumental differ again from the times of refreshing in which we live. Let us not limit the Holy One of Israel.

When the writer of these lines — before any tokens of our American awakening had appeared — was in Great Britain, he was made aware of a most remarkable movement in the religious world. The increase of endeavors to carry the Gospel to the poor, in their most abject retreats — the continual use of open-air preaching — the rise of several evangelical ministers upon whose words the multitude were disposed to hang — the services in Exeter Hall, and even the opening of Westminster Abbey, spoke of zeal on one hand, and roused attention on the other. And when he surveyed an assembly of ten thousand souls giving rapt attention, at the Surrey Gardens, to the great evangelist of our age, and discerned evidence that these multitudes, continually filling anew that vast receptacle, were drawn together, not more by the remarkable gifts of that young man, than by the fearlessness with which he declares the vengeance of God against sin, and the freshness and fullness with which he offers an accomplished salvation through Jesus Christ — the conclusion was irresistible, and was repeatedly expressed, that England also was enjoying a Revival of Religion. Accidents may vary, but the essence is the same. And, all the world over, whenever God chooses to smile upon his work, instruments will be forthcoming, in free abundance and beautiful diversity. Enlarged prayer for the spread of the Gospel among the whole human family is especially demanded at the present time, when God has touched so many hearts with desire, and manifested so great a readiness to answer.

The papers which follow, in respect to whatever concerns authorship or literature, are the merest trifles; the truths which they contain, however, are of infinite importance. It is hoped that none will be repelled by the great plainness with which some of the lessons are conveyed.

The articles respecting Seamen, Firemen, and our City Population, though apparently local in their interest, concern large and important classes, and will possibly be useful in this more permanent form.

The compositions in verse, a few of which are not original, will not, it is hoped, interrupt the continuity of the serious instruction. A single article, contributed to the series by a brother in the ministry, has been allowed to retain its place; and the lines entitled THE DOOMED MAN, hitherto published without their author's consent, and sometimes erroneously, are here given in their true text.

Republication in a volume was not thought of, still less suggested by the author; but if endeavors so unpretending can be turned to good account, in the spiritual benefit of any, he will rejoice; and he adds his prayers that this may be the result.

THE REVIVAL.

When many souls are coming to Christ at one time, we call it a Revival of Religion. There is no impropriety in this, even though the obvious effects are in converting sinners. This is always preceded by the refreshing of the Church, and just as God reneweth the face of the earth,[2] in the spring, by calling forth grass and flowers, so he revives the wintry places of his Church by bringing to light thousands of hitherto darkened souls. From Pentecost onwards, the Holy Spirit has been frequently sent in effusion so copious as to add multitudes simultaneously to the Church of such as shall be saved. O reader! a time of refreshing from the presence of the Lord is also a time for great "searchings of hearts."[3] Will you give a few moments to certain solemn and tender inquiries?

1. *Are you an enemy of the Revival?* You shudder at the thought! yet enemies there are; an arch-enemy, a liar, a murderer, the old serpent, is still the foe of Christ and all his works. His aids and emissaries seek to hinder the arousing of saints, and the conversion of sinners. Perhaps you have heard them sneer and rail at the work of grace; which they deride as a disease or an infatuation. "These people are insane." "These men are full of new wine."[4] Perhaps you have joined in the laughter of the sons of Belial; or have been afraid or ashamed to break silence. Consider with which party you then ranked yourself. "Who is on the Lord's side?"[5] is still the question. To mock at the operations of the Holy Spirit, ascribing them to lower causes, is not unlike the sin of the Pharisees, who dishonored the mir-

acles of Christ.[6]

Men may fight against God,[7] and oppose his work of grace, by denying or disparaging it; by dwelling on every person or incident which has a ludicrous side; by repressing the feelings of awakened souls; or by encouraging frivolous and distracting conversation, reading, or amusements, when the Spirit of God is clearly and mightily moving the community to solemn consideration, bitter grief for sin, and earnest turning from the world to Christ.

2. *Do you rejoice in the Revival?* The Church cries to God: Wilt thou not revive us again, that thy people may rejoice in thee? The Church has no greater joy on earth; yea, the Church in heaven rejoices over one sinner that repenteth;[8] God and Christ rejoice over multitudes renewed and forgiven. Is this your joy, O reader? When the mighty awakening took place in the region of Samaria, "there was great joy in that city."[9] One converted family is cause of joy; when a whole church, when a whole neighborhood, when multitudes in a city, turn unto the Lord, how exceedingly great should be the gladness of all who love Christ and love souls! Are you conscious of such joy? Can it be a matter of indifference to a truly renewed soul, even to hear a report of hundreds brought to confess the Lord Jesus? Feel as Christ and holy angels feel, and you will possess a joy in the salvation of fellow-creatures and the glory of your Lord. But possibly you know nothing of all this.

3. *Are you a subject of the Revival?* The kingdom of God has come nigh unto you; but are you of it? You hear, perhaps you speak, of the great revival; but have you been yourself revived? Has your cold heart, dead in trespasses and sins, been made alive by the Spirit of the living God? "Dost thou believe on the Son of God?"[10] Have old things passed away, and have all things become new?[11] Have you

that love to the Lord Jesus Christ, without which your sentence is ANATHEMA MARANATHA?[12] Have you crucified the flesh, with the affections and lusts?

These are very serious questions, to which you have long since given a deliberate answer, if you have been faithful to your own soul. Believe me, dear reader, it is not enough to be a communicant in the church. Thousands have been such, who are now in hell. A revived church possesses revived members. Are you such a one? Lay the hand on the breast and say, has the pervading influence of the blessed Spirit kindled your soul to new faith, hope, love, devotion, and duty? If not, you are still outside of this shower of grace.

4. *Do you pray for the Revival?* Many thousands are so praying. It began in prayer. This fresh gift of the loving Saviour was born amidst the cries and tears of his people. While they were speaking, God was near, to bless. Thus he came upon the gathered Eleven, and thus upon the pentecostal meeting for prayer.[13] The precept is still in force. Pray for the peace of Jerusalem; the promise still holds good, "They shall prosper that love thee."[14] As revivals begin in prayer, so are they maintained by prayer. The minister of the Word is but a fainting Moses, if Aaron and Hur cease to uphold his hands.[15] If we would see many thousands converted to God, we must pray. "For thus saith the Lord God, I will yet for this be inquired of by the house of Israel to do it for them; I will increase them with men like a flock; as the holy flock, as the flock of Jerusalem in her solemn feasts."[16] In the house of God, in the converted meeting of brethren, in the Sunday-school, in the family, in the closet, pray, pray, pray!

5. *Are you helping forward the Revival?* There is much work to be done among saints and sinners. Almighty God is the only effectual power. Paul and Apollos are nothing,

till God give the increase. Yet men are coworkers with God; humble instruments to convey his truth and promote his glory. Say not you are weak. He hath chosen the weak things of this world to confound the mighty. Say not you have no influence; you have already exerted too much, on the wrong side. Go forward in the name of the Lord, with light and love, and you shall be- hold the fruit of your labor. You have a relative, a partner, a friend, a dependant, a neighbor, whose soul you have neglected. You have an hour in the week, or five minutes in the day, which you have failed to devote to saving an immortal being. You may conduct one to a religious meeting; you may bless another by rebuke. You may lend a book, give a tract, write an affectionate letter. Especially you may plead with some fellow-creature, that he would be reconciled to God. Peradventure your working-time is short.

6. *Does your heart care for the fruits of the Revival?* There is a duty to the golden sheaves after the ears have fallen before the sickle. Folded sheep must be watched and fed. New converts are endangered creatures, lambs amidst wolves. Christ cares for them, and wills that his servants should care for them. It is not the will of the Father that one of these little ones should perish.[17] Beware how you offend, that is, betray into sin, one of these little ones. Seek to prevent their straying. Seek to imbue them with sound doctrine. This ductile condition is the very one in which to receive the mould of truth.[18] Earnestly endeavor to bring them to an intelligent and sincere profession of faith, and then to useful labors. Half the benefit of revivals is lost from neglect of those who have been converted. Might not classes of instruction for such persons, after the primitive model, be found valuable? Dear Christian reader, if your heart has ever felt true penitence and love to Jesus, feed his sheep, feed his lambs!

7. *Have you sought to honor God in the Revival?* The glory of God the Saviour is the chief end to be regarded, in the salvation of the perishing. Every true conversion adds splendor to Messiah's crown. By every true revival of religion, glory redounds to the Lord God Almighty. But this declarative glory is lessened by every thing in the work which overclouds divine grace, or exalts poor, sinful man, and his doings and deservings. Oh! how careful should he be, in every meeting, in every devotion, in every word, to maintain a reverence and godly fear for that Holy One whom we profess to believe present! "For our God is a consuming fire."[19] The young Levite, who unwarily touched the ark, was zealous but not reverent. When dealing with or for souls, we can not be too gentle and tender, even as a nurse cherisheth her [own] children; we can not be too humble and meek. Pray for the 'love of the Spirit.'[20] Shun all that is censorious, or savoring of spiritual pride. All religious experiences are doubtful, which leave the soul arrogant, unteachable, harsh, and denunciatory. Let the awe of God's presence affect us, as it did the seraphim; and when our exultation is highest, let us most deeply cry: HOLY, HOLY, HOLY![21] How tenderly we should fear lest any uncrucified tempers of ours, should 'eat as doth a canker,' and spread contagion through the blessed work.[22] So live, beloved brother in the Lord, that you may be able to say of all around you, as did Paul, "And they glorified God in me."[23]

FOR REVIVAL.

Behold thy drooping vine, O God!
And shed thy quickening grace abroad;
Our graces faint, our joys decline.
Yet still, Redeemer, we are thine.

Awake to help us from on high,
And let delivering power be nigh,
Hear our bewailings and complaints,
And grant revival to thy saints.

As in the times of old come down,
And cease in just rebuke to frown:
Far we have wandered from thy way,
Arrest us lest we further stray.

By thy convincing power reprove,
And wake the sleepers into love,
Cause us again to hear the sound
Of anxious moanings all around.

We suppliant plead in that great Name,
Which saves thy heritage from shame;
For Jesus' sake display thy power,
In this our dark and sinking hour.

SEEK TO SAVE SOULS.

God only can save a soul, in the high and proper sense. It is He who converts the sinner. Yet in Scripture human instruments are said to convert and save.[24] The motives to attempt this, are regard for the glory of God, and love to the souls of men. In seasons of religious revival, both principles are operative in numbers of believers. Reader, pause and ask yourself, how it is with you?

To be the instrument of converting a single soul, is so great a blessing and honor, that if there were no other way to accomplish it, any true Christian would be willing to lay down his life. "He which converteth the sinner from the error of his way, shall save a soul from death, and shall hide a multitude of sins."[25] Think thus: With God's blessing, I shall save this soul from death; I shall glorify God by hiding all this sinner's transgressions. At times, when the hearing ear is given to many; when your neighbors are accessible; when inquiry is wide-spread; and when the very rumor of wonderful conversions startles the once careless, oh! be up and doing! The greatness of the work can not be overrated. If you have done nothing yet towards saving a soul, you have that before you which exceeds in glory all that you have hitherto accomplished in your whole life. And if every professing Christian in our churches were rightly affected on this subject, we might expect to see efforts beyond all that the world has witnessed. Such awakenings and harvests would come, as in our present unbelief we hardly dare to pray for. If great and unexampled ingatherings of souls ever bless our world, as Christians pray and hope they may, these will doubtless be preceded by a spirit of individual earnestness in bringing sinners to Christ. Such a temper is inseparable from the new nature. No sooner does a believer taste that the Lord is gracious, than he desires, yea longs, to make his excellency known to others. His language to all around is: "Come and hear, all ye that fear God, and I will declare what He hath done for my soul."[26] Such is the law of progress in the kingdom. "When Andrew hears John, and follows the Redeemer, see how he instantly goes in pursuit of his brother Simon, and brings him to Jesus. When Philip, the townsman of these disciples, has been called by the Lord, he instantly seeks to bring in Nathaniel.[27] Christian reader, whom have you sought and found? What straying sheep, lost among thorns and wolves, have you ever brought back? Is it not high time to consider this duty and privilege?

A soul — a soul — an immortal soul! Think of its capacity, its duration, its value I Think of the hell it must endure, if impenitent; of the heaven it shall possess, if pardoned. Think of the price laid down by the incarnate Son of God. "What shall it profit a man if he gain the whole world, and lose his own soul; or what shall a man give in exchange for his soul?"[28] These considerations will incite you to new efforts towards convincing and persuading sinners. O my brother! though your endeavors should be blessed to the saving of only one, what will be the reward of meeting that one in heaven!

There is powerful motive in the peril of the unconverted. Reflect, that the very arguments by which we try to work conviction in sinners, are equally valid to work in us zeal for their salvation. Do preachers and friends urge on them that they are under God's awful wrath and curse? The same reason should impel us to pluck them as brands out of the burning. Are they every moment exposed to the damnation of hell? Then not a moment should we leave them in this jeopardy. Is it a horrible thing for sinners to be at enmity with God, and devoid of all love for our blessed Jesus? This is an unanswerable reason why we should pray and speak and labor, that they may be reconciled and saved. If we strongly believe the truth, and ardently love our fellow-men, we shall let no opportunity slip, of throwing divine lessons into their minds; nay, we shall devise and make opportunities, if such do not offer themselves.

Dear fellow-disciples, how far we fall below that law of souls which glowed in the Apostle of the Gentiles! He longed to win men to Christ. "I have made myself servant unto all," says he, "that I might gain the more."[29] And again: "I am made all things to all men, that I might by all means save some." Few of us sympathize with his tears, shed while he wrote of the impenitent. "Many walk," so he addressed the Philippians, "of whom I have often told you, and now tell you even weeping, that they are the enemies of the cross of Christ."[30] Can we really believe what we say of our unconverted friends? Are they truly "strangers from the covenants of promise, having no hope, and without God in the world"?[31] Surely, there is some secret skepticism which palsies the sinews of our exertion. Did we inwardly and heartily believe what we profess, we should be calling upon the ungodly all around us, to turn to God. The heathen mariners exclaimed to Jonah: "What meanest thou, O sleeper? arise! call upon thy God!"[32] Much more, if convinced that they are perishing, should we strive to alarm the guilty conscience of careless companions. What would be our course if a neighbor were discovered to be in danger of losing his life? Suppose a case. One whom you esteem is sleeping in a house which you know to be in flames. Or a beloved young friend is embarking on a vessel which you know is not seaworthy. Or a person near and dear to you is about to be waylaid by assassins. You know what would be your acts in such a juncture. But, oh! inconsistent brother! you behold an infinitely greater danger; yet you do nothing! You are as uncertain of this friend's life, as of your own. The death of either will frustrate the plan now proposed to you. Before he is summoned to the awful bar of God, make some attempt to save his soul. Of such activity as this, we may say without hesitation: "Whatsoever thy hand findeth to do, do it with thy might; for there is no work, nor device, nor knowledge, nor wisdom in the grave, whither thou goest."[32] All exhortations and entreaties, to ungodly fellow-creatures, must be during the present life. And as you have sometimes feared for yourself, lest the Spirit of God should be quenched, and your day of grace overclouded, so ought you to fear for them. How knowest thou, O Christian! but that the intercession has been only for a year, a month, or a day, in the case of your friend; and that even Jesus has said: "After that, thou shalt cut it down"?[33] Peradventure, while you linger about this obvious piece of faithfulness, the just Judge is saying to the sinner: "Thou fool, this night thy soul shall be required of thee!"[34]

How solemn is the reflection, and how should it press you forward to instant act, that many whom you might have addressed on this topic, are now beyond your reach. Sit down and ponder, as you recall the past. 'There was M., who lived months in my house, yet to whom I never recommended my Lord. She is now in a foreign land, afar from all evangelical means. There is N., who was misled by my worldliness and fashionable folly. She has died without hope. There is young P.; my lips were half-opened to warn him; but it is too late; he has been driven away in his wickedness.'[35] Shall such events be occurring every day, and yet shall disciples of Jesus refrain from seeking to save souls? O reader! bring the claim home to your own conscience! Can you sleep tonight, without having tried to save a soul from death? Who is he, to whom you will address yourself? Go to your closet, and cry mightily unto God for his blessing on the weak endeavor. Then set about it, in tender love. It may be only a sentence, broken with sobs, yet it may go to the heart. It may be a book, a tract, a passage of Scripture, a hymn; each of these has proved the arrow from God's bow. Above all, an affectionate and faithful letter to an unconverted acquaintance is often the very message to be owned of the Spirit.

You have neglected souls! Your conduct has said: "Am I my brother's keeper?"[36] You have practically avowed the principle: "Go! serve other gods!"[37] Many there are, who are tempted to exclaim: "No man cared for my soul."[38] What words can depict the horrors of the case, where the impenitent person, thus neglected and thus liable to God's wrath, is bone of your bone, and flesh of your flesh![40] Shall a man allow the wife of his bosom to hear no more from him concerning salvation than if he were a corpse? O hardened soul! shall thy husband perish without a word from thy lips? And who shall care for the souls of children, if their parents do not? There is not a family, a bank, a ship, a counting-house, a factory, a shop, a place of business, a school, in which these counsels have not direct application. He or she, whom you see every day, who is next to you, and who doubtless wonders at your cowardly silence, is the very person to whom you should speak.

Thousands of thousands are yet to love Jesus, and reflect his image. If some of these shall have been brought to glory by your means, what an honor and delight! Eminently faithful men and women have been the instruments of rescuing many. "And they that be wise, shall shine as the brightness of the firmament; and they that turn many to righteousness, as the stars forever and ever."[41]

UTTERANCE.

If God the Lord will show to me
   The glory of his grace,
My lips shall speak the promise free
   Out in the holy place.

Let the live coal my lips refine,
   And love inspire my heart,
Then my glad voice shall loudly join,
   The blessing to impart.

When guilt lies heavy on the soul,
   The preacher's voice is weak,
But joy can gush without control,
   And bursting love can speak.

'Tis utterance from within that finds,
   Its way to hearts of stone.
And Christ's own Spirit melts the minds
   When mercy breathes the tone.

PRAY FOR THE SPIRIT.

In order to mighty and unexampled revival, what we especially need is for the whole Church to be down on its knees before God. Past redemptions should make our cravings great. "I am the Lord thy God, which brought thee out of the land of Egypt; open thy mouth wide, and I will fill it."[42] Thousands have already been seen gathered in one place for prayer, but when "the Spirit of grace and of supplications" is poured out on the great body of Christians, touched with pity for the desolations of the spiritual Jerusalem, that word will come true: "Thou shalt arise and have mercy upon Zion, for the time to favor her, yea, the set time is come; for thy servants take pleasure in her stones, and favor the dust thereof."[43] Oh! that God's people were awake to the privilege of crying aloud for his great gift!

Open your mind, believing reader, to the extraordinary truth, that God has an infinite willingness to bestow in answer to prayer that which, since the sending of his Son, is the greatest of all his possible gifts. "If ye then, being evil, know how to give good gifts unto your children, how much more shall your Heavenly Father give THE HOLY SPIRIT to them that ask him?"[44] O parent! ponder on this blessed verse; there is that within thy heart which will reveal its meaning! And what is it that God is so ready to give? It is that which secures and applies all the benefits of Christ's mediation; that which makes revivals here, and heaven hereafter; it is the HOLY SPIRIT! Ought not all disciples, all over the world, to be prostrate before the throne of grace, beseeching God for Christ's sake to communicate this all-comprehensive boon? To him only do we look, because with him is "the residue of the Spirit."[45] But we ask in the name of CHRIST, for the very name means *Anointed*, and the anointing, which flows from him as Head, to all the members, is this very gift, the Holy Ghost, "for God giveth not the Spirit by measure unto him."[46] He hath it immeasurably, and for his Church, and they draw for it in his name by prayer. Occupy a few moments upon this great gift; it will aid your prayers.

1. There is such a thing as the pouring out of the Holy Ghost. As Moses "poured of the anointing oil on Aaron's head," so God pours the unction of his Spirit on the head of our Great High Priest.[47] And as the ceremonial fragrance flowed down to "the skirts of his garments,"[48] so the gift of the Spirit comes on all believers. "The anointing which ye have received of him," says the Apostle John, "abideth in you."[49] But the effusion is sometimes uncommonly great, even to outpouring. Some have found fault with the term, which nevertheless is intensely biblical, and consecrated in the Church. Among promises to Israel in the latter day, the Lord says: "Neither will I hide my face any more from them; for I have poured out my Spirit upon the house of Israel, saith the Lord God."[50] Apostolic comment applies to New Testament times the words of another prophet: "I will pour out my Spirit upon all flesh."[51] So in another place: "Behold, I will pour out my Spirit unto you."[52] The idea necessarily presented is that of bountiful effusion. Let us ask for it. The Lord Jesus comforted his sorrowing disciples by the promise of this gift, as the result of his ascension. "If I depart, I will send him unto you."[53] This Comforter he did send, O! how graciously and gloriously, at the first Christian Pentecost. *"Having received of the Father the promise of the Holy Ghost,"* said the Apostle Peter, "he hath shed forth this which ye now see and hear."[54] There had just been suddenly a sound from heaven, as of a rushing mighty wind, filling all the house where they were sitting; "and they were all filled with the Holy Ghost." Do not fail to observe, that believers had been in union of prayer for this very gift, thus complying with the Lord's injunction that they should " wait for the promise of the Father."[55] The gift was continued, under early preaching; and "the Holy Ghost fell on them that heard the Word."[56] The same Apostle, many years afterwards, refers to the known fact of "the Holy Ghost sent down from heaven."[57] Every great awakening and plentiful harvest of souls has proceeded from the same Spirit, sought by the same importunity of beseeching prayer. Therefore, pray for the Spirit!

2. *The influence of the Holy Spirit of God is exceedingly powerful*. We ask something mighty and revolutionizing. It is Omnipotence that we are praying for. A wicked city, a wicked world, will yield to no inferior strength. What an encouragement that "with the Lord Jehovah is everlasting strength!" It is as applicable to revival of the Church as to the rebuilding of the Temple. "Not by might, nor by power, but by my Spirit, saith the Lord of hosts."[58] Let Christians no longer despair of the conversion of high-handed sinners, even the vilest of the vile, in our filthiest and bloodiest dens; as if we expected in answer to our prayers only some weak, half-way operation. "Our gospel," says the Apostle of the Gentiles, "came not unto you in word, only, but also in power, *and in the Holy Ghost*, and in much assurance."[59] This is our ground of hope when the ministers of the Word proclaim the glad tidings; that the preaching may be "in demonstration of the Spirit and of power."[60] God grant us deliverance from our unbelief, as to the power of the Holy Spirit in giving efficacy to the truth!

3. *The Spirit, whom we seek, is the Author of*

Regeneration and Sanctification. If God vouchsafe us these, in wide extent, our revival will be indeed complete. "That which is born of the Spirit is spirit."[61] All believers shout the same praise: "According to his mercy he saved us, by the washing of regeneration, and renewing of the Holy Ghost."[62] Look at thousands, utterly blind as to spiritual realities, and say, what can we ask for them so indispensably important, as that Spirit of Truth, who will "reprove," or convince "the world of sin, and of righteousness, and of judgment?"[63] He is just as able to convert the ruffian, or the fallen woman, as the church-going Pharisee; just as able to renew a thousand as one. Who is sufficiently awake to the necessity of imploring God to convert a multitude of sinners?

All revival of the Church is increased sanctification; and all reclaiming of the impenitent is sanctification begun. For both we need the gift of the Spirit; and we need it now. We need it to break the power of sin in professing Christians, and to nail their lusts to the cross; for it is by this influence that we "do mortify the deeds of the body."[64] Some of the primitive believers had been atrocious sinners; "but," says the Apostle Paul, "ye are washed, but ye are sanctified, but ye are justified, in the name of the Lord Jesus, and by the Spirit of our God."[65] Hope, Joy, Love, and consequent activity and success, are fruits of the same Spirit.[66] In a word, the Spirit of God is the Spirit of Revival. Earnest, daily, united prayer of the people of Christ for this high gift puts honor upon God in a remarkable degree; and we already have cause to note how signally he blesses endeavors which were openly begun in prayer. Beloved brethren, let us not mistake the token, nor fail to go in the path pointed out by Providence and the Spirit.

4. *The Holy Spirit sends those gifts which are necessary for successful work.* "When miraculous gifts were

necessary, they were not withheld. All inspiration, wisdom, and ministry are from the same source. So also are the common qualifications for service demanded in the daily walk of an earnest Christian, who seeks to save souls. "There are diversities of operations, but it is the same God which worketh all in all; but the manifestation of the Spirit is given to every man to profit withal."[67] The Lord promised that the Spirit should prompt his disciples when arraigned.[68] Equally does the blessed Monitor fill their hearts and lips for common service. Apostles themselves sought for "utterance" by means of prayer;[69] and a praying Church will have a ministry and members, bold and loving in owning and recommending their Lord. The supplications, which bring down such influences, are themselves wrought of God, when believers, keeping themselves in the love of God, are at the same time "praying in the Holy Ghost."[70] See thus how completely dependent we are for all upon the Holy Spirit of God. Grace manifestly began the work; grace keeps it alive; grace must carry it on and give it extension.

Brethren, we must pray as we have never yet prayed. Our want of success is due to our coldness of desire and niggardliness of request. We are not straitened in God, but in our own low, slender conceptions and hopes. We have not, because we ask not. If we were under a deep and solemn impression of the Divine power, bounty, and faithfulness, "how should one chase a thousand, and two put ten thousand to flight!"[71] The lesson which the Revival should teach us is the duty of being instant in supplication for the larger and more glorious effusion of the Holy Spirit. Acting on this, we shall behold new marvels of love in the place of prayer.

FOR SINCERITY.

Master, when I attempt thy work,
A thousand vexing cares are nigh,
A thousand base corruptions lurk,
To make me linger, fall or fly:
More than thy orders, Lord, I need,
For constant strengthening grace I plead.

When I should seek thy only praise,
Wretch! I am seeking oft my own;
Nor can I hymns of glory raise
Devoutly at thy sacred throne,
But that the self-exalting strain
Intrudes to make my worship vain.

Oft when my lips express a care
For what concerns thy work alone,
Among the musings, cluster there
Some little troubles of my own;
Self still has place, alas! I fear
'Tis self that speaks and governs here.

Yet if thy glory thou reveal —
If Christ in full effulgence shine —
If heavenly rapture o'er me steal —
And love, and joy, and zeal combine—
The new emotions shall expel
The retinue of sin and hell.

THE UNAWAKENED

Unawakened! Alas, O sinner! unless thou be awakened, thou must perish!

Not long ago, a house containing many inmates was burned down at night. Several persons perished in the flames. Would you know the reason? They were awakened too late. So the finally impenitent sinner will awake; but too late! Those are dreadful words, even in some earthly conjunctures. TOO LATE! TOO LATE! You stand by the brink of a deep and rapid river, and see a youth fall into its waters. He sinks, struggling, and then rises. Boats put out; gallant fellows pull to his rescue; they seize his tangled hair as he rises once more, and bear his drenched and flaccid body to the bank. It is too late! The breath of life has fled. So in many conceivable instances of earthly peril, in some of which the perishing creature, a suicide for example, awakes to the direful truth of his catastrophe; but awakes too late! Sinner, you will assuredly awake, either in time or in eternity.

Sooner or later, a man's sins find him out."[72] Perhaps in temporal disgrace and retribution. Perhaps at the hour of death. Beyond all peradventure at the bar of God. The rich man was not awakened in his purple and fine linen. In his lifetime he received his good things; but "in hell he lift up his eyes, being in torments." He was then fully awake. Can you endure the thought of being aroused by your sins, where no pardons are vouchsafed?

"There are no acts of pardon past
In the cold grave to which we haste;
But darkness, death, and long despair
Reign in eternal silence there."

"It is high time to awake out of sleep." These words are as applicable to this case, as to that intended by the Apostle. Oh! for a trumpet-blast, loud enough to startle the careless reader of these words into a salutary fear of death, judgment and eternal wrath! You walk on the brink of a precipice, and God's holiness, justice, and truth are all against you. Yet it is your offended Judge who continues to pursue you with the cry: "Behold, now is the accepted time: behold now is the day of salvation."[73] The time is auspicious. It is God's time. "To-day, if ye will hear his voice, harden not your hearts."[74] To-morrow has no promises. To-morrow you may be in eternity. Death has surprised thousands at the very time when they were procrastinating repentance. The foolish virgins were not awakened till they heard the midnight cry: "Behold, the bridegroom cometh!" The voice of the archangel and the trump of God will wake every sleeper, for "all that are in the graves shall hear His voice, and shall come forth; they that have done good, unto the resurrection of life, and they that have done evil, unto the resurrection of damnation."[75] Is it not astonishing that you can hear such things from the lips of Him who so loved the world as to die for it, and that you should still remain unmoved?

Be convinced, careless reader, that there is nothing so unreasonable as to remain unawakened, when called by Almighty God. Awakening truths come near on every side, sounding from heaven, earth, and hell. There are cases in which fear is unreasonable, but this is not one of them. No man can rationally despise the "wrath of the Lamb." He who dies in his sins, dies in rejection of the only sacrifice for sin. The dread of so dying ought to take hold of your heart while you read. Those terrible denunciations against sinners, from which they turn away, lest conscience should be shaken from its slumber, proceed not from the mouth of a harsh, malignant being, but from the meek and lowly Jesus, who weeps over lost souls. It ought to prove a pungent consideration that of all the expressions which Scripture contains concerning everlasting wo, the most fearful are those which fell from the gentle lips of Jesus. A little searching of the sacred volume will show this to be true. The Redeemer spake these threatenings in love, and the thought of this should break the dream of indolent security. Christ's terrors are meant to alarm you out of your sins and your false confidence, and so to make way for His tender mercies. But his mercies are exhibited to the unreconciled only in the present life; and your tenure of human existence, fellow-sinner, is very slight and precarious.

To remain unawakened is madness itself, unless the Omniscient can be evaded, and the Omnipotent set at nought. "Be not deceived; God is not mocked; for whatsoever a man soweth, that shall he also reap."[79] Beware, lest God, long put off and thrust aside, swear in his wrath that you shall not enter into his rest. The downfall of the secure is sometimes precipitous. "He that, being often reproved, hardeneth his neck, shall suddenly be destroyed, and that without remedy." This hardening is produced by a continued process of hearing God's call without heeding it. How knowest thou, O sinner! but that the sentence hath already gone forth against thee: " Cut it down; why cumbereth it the ground?" There is a point at which Mercy, after many pleadings for the impenitent soul, stands aside and suffers Justice to take its course. Continued and obdurate resistance to the blood of the Lord Jesus, is no venial sin in the sight of God. They who reject this Mediator need look for no other. "Let us therefore fear, lest, a promise being left us of entering into his rest, any of you should seem to come short of it." That measure of concern for sin, of which you are conscious while you read these words, is caused by the Spirit of God. Take heed how you trifle with this monition. The sacred fire within may, by your neglect or transgression, have been reduced to a single coal; a single beam of light touching your ruined state may glimmer within. "QUENCH NOT THE SPIRIT." There are critical moments in every biography; instants on which are suspended heaven and hell. Every lost soul has had a last call. There is a possibility that this is yours. . Therefore resist not the Holy Ghost.[80] How awful the moment in which an immortal spirit is left of God! The victim of impenitent procrastination may be as little aware of his doom, as was Samson when "he wist not that the Lord was departed from him." What though no cloud of holy angels be seen with averted faces slowly to return from their watch beside the sinner? What though no muttering thunder rolls its portentous signal of wo along the horizon? What though no gigantic scales, held out from high heaven, bear the inscription: "Mene, thou art weighed in the balances and art found wanting." The deed is nevertheless done; the book of divine offers is closed; the last whisper of gospel persuasion has died away. For some, this epoch coincides with the instant of dying. Who shall say, that for others it may not fall in with some earlier moment of life? The very hint of such a possibility might well electrify the stupid heart. Do not say there need be no haste, but go, O lingerer! to thy knees! and, bewailing thy impenitent mind, yield thyself to God.

To be unawakened, is the more sinful and hazardous, at a time like this, when the community is moved, even the heart of the people, "as the trees of the wood are moved with the wind." Is the Great King among us, of a truth? Then is it time for every living soul to be up and doing. Think you the blind, the halt, the maimed, the palsied and the leprous lay asleep, when the Son of David was passing through the highways of Galilee and Judea on his errands of mercy? As little should the ungodly be sunk in apathy when the Lord, by His Spirit, is putting forth awakening energy in our churches. He who slumbers through such shakings, dishonors God and endangers his own soul. To go untouched through an extensive revival of religion, is to be distinguished in a fearful way. Thus we have seen the tall "trunk blackened and scathed by lightning, rearing itself among the trees of the forest. Is it your case, dear reader? You have listened cold and hard to the Word of God, which has been to others "as a fire, and like a hammer, that breaketh the rock in pieces."1 You have been present during devotions, in which the hearts of believers have flowed like molten gold. You have been singled out for the prayers of the church; but you have wrought mightily against those prayers, by your hard and impenitent heart. If you perish after all, it will not be by the common lot of the lost.

Consent to meditate, to consider, and to return. Our hope of this result leads us to address even the hardened: "If peradventure God will give them repentance to the acknowledging of the truth; and that they may awake themselves out of the snare of the devil, who are taken captive by him at his will."[81]

There is a time, we know not when,
A point, we know not where.
That marks the destiny of men
To glory or despair.

There is a line, by us unseen,
That crosses every path;
The hidden boundary between
God's patience and his wrath.

To pass that limit is to die,
To die as if by stealth;
It does not quench the beaming eye,
Or pale the glow of health.

The conscience may be still at ease,
The spirits light and gay;
That which is pleasing still may please,
And care be thrust away.

But on that forehead God has set,
Indelibly, a mark,
Unseen by man, for man as yet
Is blind and in the dark.

And yet the doomed man's path below,
Like Eden, may have bloomed;
He did not, does not, will not know
Or feel that he is doomed.

Ho knows, he feels, that all is well,
And every fear is calmed:
He lives, he dies, he wakes in hell,
Not only doomed, but damned.

Oh! where is this mysterious bourne,
By which our path is crossed;
Beyond which God himself hath sworn
That he who goes is lost?

How far may we go on in sin?
How long will God forbear?
Where does hope end? and where begin
The confines of despair?

An answer from the skies is sent:
"Ye that from God depart!
While it is called to-day, repent!
And harden not your heart."

HARDEN NOT YOUR HEART.

1. THERE is such a thing as vaguely admitting a statement to be true, and yet not receiving it so as to act upon it. This is practical unbelief. A man is in the habit of using intoxicating drinks without restraint. His medical adviser lays before his eyes an old age of decrepitude, pain, or palsy. His spiritual adviser points out to him the impending evil of drunkenness. He is to a certain extent convinced, but his practice remains the same. One who labors under an insidious disease, is told that unless immediate means be used, it will probably prove fatal. He half believes, but flatters himself, and goes on as before. A rash adventurer in merchandise is warned that his speculation will end in bankruptcy; yet he pushes forward and runs upon the catastrophe. These are familiar instances. But still more common and still more deplorable is the same blindness in regard to eternal realities. The sinner admits that he is unprepared to die and in peril of eternal wrath; and if he believed this with the power of his mind, he would be convulsed with agony. But there is nothing influential in his vague persuasions, and therefore they do not deserve the name of faith. Thus he hardens his heart.

2. Men are kept from believing by their supposed interests, prejudices, and passions. This is an admitted principle in the philosophy of evidence, recognized in all legislation and jurisprudence. Why is a man deemed incompetent to decide in a case which involves his own interest? Not merely because it is feared he will deliber-

ately judge against his sincere convictions of the truth; this were a shallow and superficial explanation; but because his bias will actually influence him to believe what is untrue. Twelve men in a jury-box hear precisely the same evidence; yet one of them, who is secretly but deeply concerned, hears all at a disadvantage, and comes to a conclusion adverse to the truth of the case. Which of us is able with perfect candor to credit testimony against his own child as freely as against a stranger? Here is a wide field for the operation of our inborn depravity, in hardening the heart against the truth of God. By a perverse abstraction, we hear all on one side. We lend an ear to that part of the evidence and argument which is favorable to what we have predetermined. We are deaf to reasons on the other part, which, to a mind not preoccupied, would be demonstrative.

3. Closely connected with this is the power which the mind has of turning itself away from that which is unpleasant. The edge of the thoughts may be averted, first from the testimony or the reasons, and then from the partially admitted truth. We may withhold our attention, or bestow it upon something else. It is not enough that truth be held before the mind for an instant. There must be consideration, in order to influence the will and the life. Momentary flashes of belief are ineffectual. The seal must not only touch, but for a season abide upon the waxen surface. Religious truth is robbed of its power when the mind refuses to ponder on it; and then the heart is hardened. Many an urgent message of God's Word strikes with a ray of conviction, but the mind shrinks and, as it were, closes its eyes. For this voluntary exclusion the soul is of course deeply responsible. These acts are repeated thousands of times during an impenitent life.

4. But perhaps the most common method of hardening

the heart, and that to which the words of the text are most specially directed, is that of procrastination. The mind for a moment admits the truth and puts it off. This is precisely the same in its effects as deliberate rejection. Often repeated, it becomes a habit of the soul, and effectually prevents salvation. The resolution not to hear God now is involved in the resolution to hear at some other time. What is postponed to-day, will be more easily postponed to-morrow, and so life slips away. Old age is more enslaved by the evil habit than childhood and youth. Thus the arch-enemy gains his point; the heart is hardened and the door of mercy is allowed to close. And it is the destructive influence of this treacherous temper, which is opposed by the words of the Holy One crying in our ears: "*To-day,* if ye will hear his voice, harden not your hearts!"

Let me call the reader's attention to this part of the solemn admonition.

1. TO-DAY then is the best time for opening the heart to divine impressions, because it is God's time. He is a sovereign, and it is wonderful that he should treat with us at all; but when he does so, we must surely admit his authority to fix his own time. Especially when the communication to which he asks our response is one of abounding mercy. He demands the heart now; he offers pardon and renewal now. If it is ignominious to disregard the entreaties of a friend, how guilty are those who turn away from the beseechings of their God and Saviour! If we were to treat the proposals of a fellow-mortal in this manner he would leave our doors and shake off the dust of his feet against us. Is there no malignity then in the sin of asking God, our offended Lord, to await our good pleasure? He knocks, but the hard heart will not admit him.

2. TO-DAY is the time, because tomorrow the heart will he harder. Delay increases the indisposition to return.

The conscience acquires armor, and becomes skilled to ward off the sword of the Spirit. The history of every soul shows this to be true; your own case shows it. There have been days, and memory recalls them well, in which you had no peace by reason of your sins. You thought of little else for a season; you read and prayed and strove. Those days are far away in the distant past. Scripture and sermons and providential warnings find you less penetrable than you were. Should not this warn you against further procrastination? You complain that it is difficult to yield yourself unreservedly to God. Oh! betray not your souls by the belief that delay will make it less difficult. There are those in whom the disposition to defer divine subjects has become from habit almost a part of their nature. They are steeled against every weapon, for long continuance in an evil way has made the heart hard, and there is nothing they regard so little as the voice of God.

3. *Harden not the heart* TO-DAY, because to-morrow *the number and aggravation of your sins will be increased;* and they will go on increasing. Are they not sufficiently numerous? and is not their crimson hue sufficiently deep? If you could bring yourself to call them up in order, you would soon be overwhelmed. Is it not the exquisite painfulness of this survey which causes you to resist the light? Be not deceived. Remorse will overtake you, either in this world or in that which is to come. You do but act the part of an unthrifty debtor, who avoids settlement and plunges yet more deeply towards his ruin. Every new page in the book of God's account adds to the wrath and terror of your future reckoning. Most who read this have already lived the greater part of their time on earth, and some are very near the great tribunal. During all this period there has been an accumulation of guilt — mountains of unpardoned sin. Why should you add to the dreadful mass?

TO-DAY, God comes with offers of pardon. TO-DAY, if ye will hear his voice, he is ready to be reconciled. Though you have repeatedly refused him, yet to-day he is willing to enter into your heart. Why should he find it locked against him? Why will you continue to offend, and add transgression to transgression? Consider, moreover, from this time forward your acts of disobedience acquire an additional quality of turpitude; for they will be committed against clearer light and newer mercies, after fresh strivings of the Spirit, and with deeper wounds of conscience. And the oftener you have been ineffectually wrought upon by divine considerations, the more direct will be your opposition to the truth, and the more heinously culpable the hardening of your heart.

4. TO-DAY is the only safe time, for *to-morrow you may he in eternity.* Life is uncertain. "Boast not thyself of to-morrow, for thou knowest not what a day may bring forth." "He that being often reproved hardeneth his neck, shall suddenly be destroyed, and that without remedy." Behold now is the accepted time; behold now is the day of salvation. Can you reasonably expect God to wait the movements of an impenitent heart, which perpetually renders him nothing but denials for all his proposals of grace? How dreadful would be the narrative, if I could unfold it, of those who have been summoned away in the midst of these procrastinations! The moment when they vainly promised themselves that they would open their hearts to the divine visitant, found them beyond the reach of hope. You are conscious that you stand in dread of death, and yet you madly refuse the only gift which can disarm death of his horrors. The part of wisdom is to leave nothing to hazard. The argument is so convincing that none can seriously persevere in considering it, without an increase of feeling, and hence you turn away from it — in other words,

you harden the heart. Yet I press it, earnestly and affectionately, once again, knowing that in the hand of God it has been used to bring many a rebel to his right mind. This dream of *to-morrow*, if unbroken by an unusual effort, will wrap you in its delusions until your last breath.

5. Repent TO-DAY, because *refusal so to do is inconsistent with a desire to repent.* Unconverted persons never more deceive themselves than when they plead that they have a sincere wish to return to God. If you credit their assertions, there is nothing which they so strongly desire as to have experience of true religion. But such a desire, if genuine, would instantly break up all these habits of indolent lingering. He who desires to be healed, flies to the physician. He who means to escape shipwreck, loses not a moment in lashing himself to some buoyant material. He who craves deliverance from conflagration, instantly rushes from amidst the flaming timbers. And he who longs to be saved, puts aside every other interest and engagement as unimportant, and devotes all the energies of his soul to this single point, that he may escape from the wrath to come. How remarkably do we see it exemplified, when any man is under conviction of sin. Away with all indifference or carnal waiting, at such an hour. He reads, he prays, he looks in every direction for help, he uses every means, he thinks of nothing else. Here is a case of real desire to return to God. And the absence of all this, especially the deliberate purpose to adjourn the whole inquiry and remain longer under condemnation, is demonstrative that there is no reality of desire. Let not this hollow fallacy delude you. These are not the fruits and tokens of strong desire, and if you can plan a postponement of your greatest concern, you must have learned to harden the heart. There is no remedy but immediate acceptance of God's word.

6. Repent TO-DAY, O my hearer! let me finally urge, because *repentance is the gift of God*. You sometimes plead the difficulties of the work and your own helplessness as a reason for delay. But surely this should be mightily operative in the other direction. If God, whose voice is heard saying, *To-day, to-day,* is the only Being who can effect the great change, then you are in his sovereign hands and at his absolute mercy. If he were unwilling to receive your returning soul, he surely would not limit a certain time as the accepted period. *To-day*, we may assure you, he is ready to give repentance and remission of sins. For future days he makes no promises. Your sins are great, but he desireth not the death of the wicked. Cast yourself in absolute surrender before him whom you have offended. Throw your guilty soul into the arms of his beloved Son. Myriads now in heaven owe their salvation to this very course. Why should he urge you with his messages, and plead with you to make this the blessed moment, if there were not mercies in his heart? Why this unwonted seriousness, and this weight of solemn thought, except from influences of the Holy Spirit, who will not allow you to remain unreproved? Remember, I beseech you, that all who have become believers were once in the condition in which you now are. They felt the difficulties which you now feel. They suffered your perplexity and groped in your darkness. They were tempted to put off the day of submitting to the righteousness of God, as you are now tempted. But mark it well, they were brought to a point where further delay was impossible. And had they not been brought to this, they had never been saved. The pressure was momentous and irresistible. They were driven to this yielding. Sin was intolerable. Wrath was overhanging and insupportable. They saw before them a yawning gulf. The gleam of light on their heart and their path was so dazzling that they felt that any procrastination would be an impious aban-

doning of God. To remain in the plain of condemnation any longer they saw to be ruin. Nothing was left to them but the one determination — and they made it.

It is the voice of God your Redeemer which is sounding in your ears. Think not of him as an austere Judge, but as a compassionate Father, offering you the tender mercies of his Son. The whole work of Christ is made over to you in the offer of the Gospel for your cordial acquiescence, and that cordial acquiescence is saving faith. All is yours upon your believing. Abandon your own works and duties, your own innocence and morality, your own merits and righteousness, your own strivings, emotions, and tears. Abandon forever the vain effort to render yourselves more acceptable. Come in the one character which belongs to you, that of a corrupt, lost, and helpless sinner. Come out of yourselves, and find all in Christ. Now, while the Word is near you; now, while the seal of truth is pressed upon the somewhat yielding heart, give way to the impression and yield yourself to God. Why should not this be the happy moment, since all things are ready except your unrelenting soul? To-day, if ye will hear His voice, harden not your hearts! There will never be a freer access; there will never be a more present Saviour. The work, so long delayed, may be accomplished here and now, and your weight of sin will thenceforward be taken away wholly and forever.

VARIETIES IN ANXIOUS INQUIRY.

There are family traits in those who are born into the kingdom, but great diversity marks the individual features and expression. This may be profitably studied during a Revival of Religion. This sameness and diversity are in nothing more remarkable than in the way of coming from Satan to God; and even more particularly in the anxiety, fear, and grief of the approach. The Malefactor on the Cross and the Philippian Jailer both had their convictions, but how unlike! Saul of Tarsus and the Ethiopian courtier of Queen Candace are aroused amidst unlike circumstances. Solitary Cornelius, and the thousands at Pentecost, have remarkable resemblances and differences. The same is true of Lydia, Timothy, and other subjects of con- version named in Scripture. Inexperience

would have all converts to bear its own favorite stamp; but the Spirit of God works with a lavish, manifold, and magnificent variety, which it is our province devoutly to admire. So also it is in modern awakenings.

If we love to contemplate the unity in variety which beautifully illustrates Divine skill, power, and bounty in the kinds and species of the animal kingdom, much more should we gaze with intensity of interest upon the strange but gracious examples of spiritual operation in the saving of souls. While what is said holds good of all such operations, we may profitably confine our view to the different aspects of anxiety among inquirers.

There are some things present in almost every case of

awakening. In whatsoever place, time, or circumstances you were brought to consideration, you had a consciousness of being wrong and of being wretched. You felt yourself in danger, and believed you must do something to escape. The thought of the glorious God overhung your path, and caused you to meditate on your sins. But the degrees of this solicitude vary exceedingly; from slight ruffling of the sensibilities to utter desperation.

The man may be named, who went careless into a religious meeting, and came out with an arrow in his heart. Another has been deeply pierced by a question from a child's lips. The bare tidings of the conversion of such or such a person may bring sudden conviction to the hearer; and the report of great numbers seeking God in one place often stimulates attention, and so prostrates the sinner. Nothing is oftener blessed to this end than some sentence of the preached Word. The opening of the Bible at an unexpected place may sting a man into anguish. The word ETERNITY, at the head of a tract, is said to have smitten a fashionable sinner. One of the most eminent and long-tried saints we ever knew was brought to serious consideration in a ball- room. The late eminently pious Francis Markoe was led, not to conviction only, but to salvation, on one and the same day, in his solitary apartment; having up to this time been without any religious impressions. The convictions of St. Augustine may be read in his 'Confessions,' or in Milner. Thousands have owed their awakening to the simplest accost of a loving friend, uttered with prayer and love.

The views taken by awakened souls are different. Some are struck down as was Saul; others come gradually to a simple judgment, by no means strong at first, that they are in a wrong way of life. If a shaking, wavering conviction, the chronic trouble of common days, does not rise to acute distress in the time of Revival, it will be likely to depart without good results.

It is a great error of ignorant and inexperienced persons, to predetermine how much or how little shall be the terror and grief of a convinced soul. To determine this, is the prerogative of God. He may come in the great and strong wind, the earthquake, the fire, or in the still, small voice.[82] "Some," says the venerable annalist of the "Great Revival," in New-England, "are from the beginning carried on with abundantly more encouragement and hope than others. Some have had ten times less trouble of mind than others, in whom yet the issue seems to be the same. Some have had such a sense of the displeasure of God, and the great danger they were in of damnation, that they could not sleep; and many have said that when they lay down, the thoughts of sleeping in such a condition have been frightful to them, and they have scarcely been free from terror while they have been asleep, and have awakened with fear, heaviness, and distress, still abiding 'on their spirits. It has been very common, that the deep and fixed concern that has been on persons' minds has had a painful influence on their bodies, and given disturbance to animal nature."

The LAW OF GOD, applied to the mind and conscience, is that which works conviction. Hence the preaching of the Law precedes the preaching of the Gospel, and is indispensable. Views of the infinite Justice of God are never wanting, in sound convictions, although as to accessories and degree, these views may differ. Many who are in truth brought very low, by the convincing Spirit, are under an illusion and go about lamenting that they can not feel In others, there is a silent, but profound and immovable self-judgment, in regard to the abiding state of sin and consequent anger of God.

If we examine the direction of that wind which "bloweth where it listeth," we shall find it uniformly setting towards *self-renunciation.* "I am in the hands of a sovereign God," is the language of the sinner. The blasts of the law are driving him away from self-dependence to reliance on God.

"They that be whole need not a physician, but they that are sick."[83] He is becoming "sick" by the law; yea he is becoming "dead."[84] Hear the groaning of such a one, in his secret chamber: O Lord! help, or I perish! Without a Mediator, I am lost, lost forever. By the beams of thy holy and immutable law, I see myself depraved and guilty. The stirring up of enmity within me shows me to myself as worse, rather than better. Once I felt only my outward sins; now the rule is applied to my secret sins, my sins of purpose, sentiment, and thought, my habits and principles of sin, nay my inmost state of sin! God be merciful to me a sinner!

While to some favored souls the Lord Jesus is revealed in his plenitude of saving compassion, from the very beginning of their inquiring state; to others he seems long inaccessible. The sufferer cries: "Oh! that I knew where I might find him!" renewed convictions lead to renewed struggles. There are prayers, tears, and groans, with abundant endeavors to make the heart better, which all the while seems to grow worse. Those exercises, in which perhaps there was a certain complacency at first, lose all power of quieting the conscience. They have no merit; they give no security. So far from thinking that they are in a better way on account of these impressions and struggles, convinced souls are deeply persuaded that every additional moment of unbelief adds to the aggregate of guilt. Never before, it may be, had they such self-abhorrence and despair of self-salvation as amidst the boiling corruptions and revealed impenitence which first precedes faith and rescue. "Once," says the sinner, "I thought I had a certain amount of guilt, and I tried to wash it away. Now I see my sins innumerable, and their turpitude immeasurable. Unfit to go the fountain, I lie here on the earth, and cry, Unclean, unclean!" These are troubles out of which only Christ can deliver.

Anguish like this can not be cured by any legal performances. Indeed, the chief misery of a convinced sinner is, that he finds himself culpably unable to do the works of the law. "I have seen many," says Luther, "who have painfully travailed, and under stress of mere conscience have done the utmost that was possible, in fasts, prayers, hair-shirts, vexing and punishing the body with sundry penances, sufficient at length to destroy a frame of iron; and all to this end, that they might gain quietness and peace of conscience. Nevertheless, the more they wrought, the more were they stricken down with dread. Especially on the approach of death, some such persons, though they had lived holily, have departed with less courage than I have seen many murderers and other criminals. Therefore, it is most true, that they which do the law, do it not." But despair of help by the law conducts to the free grace of the Gospel.

The gross error of limiting the Holy Spirit to one or a few methods of working in impenitent hearts, is more common than some suppose. Among its evil consequences one is realized by inquirers themselves. Instead of following the intimations of Divine Wisdom in the Word, in respect to what are proper views and affections, they not unfrequently prescribe some way in which they are to be converted. They will hear of no other. Their predilection for this way has been derived from tradition, from uninspired books, or from common talk. All such expectations God is able to disappoint. The paths by which He leads to the Strait Gate are numberless. He who looked to be struck dumb with terror, is melted all at once by love; while, perhaps, he who meant to advance rationally, deliberately, and gradually, is transported into paroxysms of terror, which make him tremble for his reason. But all the varieties of conviction leave the soul deeply impressed with the insufficiency of every sacrifice but one. "Thou desirest not sacrifice, else would I give it; thou delightest not in burnt-offering. The sacrifices of God are a broken spirit: a broken and a contrite heart, O God! thou wilt not despise."[85]

THE SINNER'S ONLY HOPE.

"Wherewith, Lord! shall I draw near,
And bow myself before thy face?
How in thy purer eyes appear?
"What shall I bring to gain thy grace?

"Will gifts delight the Lord Most High?
Will multiplied oblations please?
Thousands of rams his favor buy,
Or slaughtered hecatombs appease?

Can these avert the wrath of God?
Can these wash out my guilty stain?
Rivers of oil, and seas of blood,
Alas I they all must flow in vain.

"Who would himself to Thee approve.
Must take the path thyself hast showed;
Justice pursue, and mercy love,
And humbly walk by faith with God.

But though my life henceforth be thine,
Present for past can ne'er atone:
Though I to thee the whole resign,
I only give thee back thine own.

Guilty I stand before thy face;
On me I feel thy wrath abide;
'Tis just the sentence should take place;
'Tis just— but oh! thy Son hath died!

LOOKING UNTO JESUS.

The words which here follow are not for the careless hardened sinner, who feels no burden; but if they should fall under the eye of one who groans beneath the weight of unpardoned iniquity, and strives to find deliverance from his pollution, then they have reached the very end for which they were destined. Let me, as it were, sit down beside this comfortless one, and, Bible in hand, point out some of its teachings concerning the way to be saved; for to the Scriptures must we go directly if we would relieve a convinced soul, who can rest in nothing short of a THUS SAITH THE LORD.

When Philip joined himself to a certain chariot, in which the Ethiopian courtier was busied over a scroll of the prophets, he found the place of Scripture to depict a *suffering Messiah.*[86] To this very point must we bring every solicitous inquirer. Beginning at that very place in Isaiah, Philip "preached unto him Jesus." It is still the only preaching which can quiet conscience and give peace. Isaiah's single prophetic picture of the Cross holds up the saving object. Look at it, as the dying Hebrew looked at the serpent on the pole! Behold the Only-Begotten, in the Garden and on the accursed tree, for thy sake. For thee, He is "a man of sorrows and acquainted with grief." He hath borne thy grief and carried thy sorrows. See Him wounded for thy transgressions, bruised for thy iniquities, laid under the chastisement of thy peace, lacerated with stripes for thy healing. Behold Him taking thy place. "He was oppressed and He was afflicted, yet he opened not His mouth; He is brought as a lamb to the slaughter, and as a sheep before her shearers is dumb, so He openeth not His mouth." See and acknowledge with faith that "the Lord hath laid on Him the iniquities of us all." "It pleased the Lord to bruise Him," to put Him to grief, to "make His soul an offering for sin." All this and more is in the single chapter which Philip expounded in the chariot. It was enough for the Ethiopian; sinner, it is enough for thee! Reject all other refuges, and come at once to the Cross.

Are you still doubting? What can satisfy you, if God's own method, in God's own message, is not enough? The entire Gospel is only a variety of ways in which to say: "Behold the Lamb of God which taketh away the sin of the world."[87] Believe that God sincerely offers to you this atonement; acquiesce in it; receive it as your own; rest and rely on it — and you are saved I

Why, O halting sinner! this delay? Why, beside the very fountain, do you proudly refuse to stoop and drink? Ah! methinks I hear you say in bitterness: "Wo is me, I am lost!" Hearken to the Word: "The Son of Man is come to seek and to save that which was lost."[88] Believe that He came to save *thee*. Again you cry: "I am chief of sinners." Again hear the Word: "This is a faithful saying, and worthy of all acceptation, that

Christ Jesus came into the world to save sinners, of whom I am chief."[89] Come, as chief of sinners, and accept that which the Apostle declares worthy of all acceptation, and therefore worthy of thine. "I am ungodly!" you rejoin; "how can God receive the ungodly?" Learn from His own answer: "Christ died for the ungodly."[90] But I am under just condemnation and curse: "Christ hath redeemed us from the curse of the law, being made a curse for us."[91] Cast your wretched soul on this truth of God, that Christ has borne your curse, when he bore your sins "in his own body on the tree." Do you still urge: "I am already doomed, as well by conscience as law, and bound over unto condign punishment?" I answer, that you are redeemed, and that God's word ought to satisfy you; redeemed "with the precious blood of Christ, as of a lamb without blemish and without spot."[92] Look to Jesus, "who His own self bare our sins in His own body on the tree."[93] "But how can I be justified in the sight of a righteous and inflexible Judge?" Read the answer in that precious word: "Being now justified by His blood."[94] No sacrifices, even of your body and life, could do it; but it is done by the blood of the Cross. Believe this.

O relenting reader! turn not away from this scene of Divine compassion, until you have taken in the full idea of what God freely offers you. There, in the Gospel of His Son, the Almighty Father makes over for your acceptance Christ and his salvation. "What I" you say; "and are all my works of legal endeavor worthless, in regard to my justification?" Yes, utterly worthless; and the sooner you reject them the better. All your doings, outward or inward, are of no merit. Such is the humbling persuasion when we receive the true Gospel; "knowing that a man is not justified by works of law, but by the faith of Jesus Christ." And if you deny this, you nullify the Cross; "for if righteousness come by the law, then Christ is dead in vain."[95] Once more you ply us with objections, such as this: "After all, the glory of Justice requires either righteousness or punishment; the righteousness I can not produce, the punishment I can not endure. Wretch that I am, I can neither obey nor propitiate!" Listen to God, rather than Satan, and receive the whole Gospel in this epitome; every word is fragrant with free grace. "Being justified freely by His grace through the redemption that is in CHRIST JESUS; whom God hath set forth to be a PROPITIATION, through faith in His blood, to declare HIS RIGHTEOUSNESS for the remission of sins that are past, through the forbearance of God; to declare, I say, His righteousness, that He might be just, and the justifier of him that believeth in Jesus."[96] How much better is one Divine saying, than all the sayings of men!

Here is a saying, O sinner I strong enough to bear the weight of thy immortal soul. True, thou art ungodly, thou hast no righteousness; but here is His righteousness, by which without ceasing to be just, that is, without ceasing to demand perfect righteousness, God can justify thee in believing. Believe, believe, then! "Believe in the Lord Jesus Christ, and thou shalt be saved."

But will so simple a thing give peace with God? Paul shall answer: "Therefore being justified by faith, we have peace with God, through our Lord Jesus Christ."[97] "And is my condemnation then reversed?" Let the same Apostle answer: "There is therefore now no condemnation to them that are in Christ Jesus."[98] Believe the testimony of God, and you are in Christ. Divine Justice beholds you in the Mediator. "If any man sin, we have an Advocate with the Father," who hath never sinned, even "Jesus Christ the righteous."[99] Think well of this verse: you have sinned, and deserved death, but Christ has never sinned, and has been "obedient unto death." This is "*His* righteousness," and may be yours, if appropriated by your faith. One glorious Redeemer has taken the place of many souls. They have no sound obedience to be righteous in, but "by the obedience of one shall many be made righteous."[100] Believe on the Lord Jesus Christ, and his righteousness is yours.

You are still reluctant, as if Jesus would not receive you, a sinner. "This man receiveth sinners."[101] "Seek from one end of the heavens to the other," says Hooker, "turn all the Bible over, and see if the words of Christ be not true. Him that cometh unto me, I will in no wise cast out." Ah! there is the point," say you; "If I were only sure that I did come!" Make sure of it, then, by believing. To "come" is to "believe." Different terms are used, but all mean one and the same taking of Jesus Christ as your Saviour, on God's free offer, which constitutes your warrant to take it. This "receiving" is explained to be the same as "believing," thus: "As many as received him, to them gave he power to become the sons of God, even to them that believe on his name."[102] When by believing you are joined to Christ, you have authority to be a child of God. Therefore, lay every thing else aside, in order to come to Christ.

The anguish of soul experienced by Martin Luther, enabled him to understand the case of anxious inquirers. To such a one he says: "When thy conscience is thoroughly afraid with the remembrance of thy sins past, when the devil assaulteth thee with great violence, going about to overwhelm thee with heaps, floods, and whole seas of sins, to terrify thee and draw thee from Christ, then arm thyself with such sentences as these: 'Christ the Son of God was given, not for the holy, righteous, worthy, and such as were his friends; but for the wicked, for sinners, for the unworthy, and for his enemies.' Wherefore if the devil say, Thou art a sinner, and therefore must be damned; then answer thou and say: 'Because thou sayest I am a sinner, therefore will I be righteous, and saved.' And if he reply, Nay, sinners must be damned, then answer and say: 'No, for I flee to Christ, who hath given himself for my sins. And therefore, Satan, in that thou sayest I am a sinner, thou givest me armor and weapons against thyself, that with thine own sword I may cut thy throat, and tread thee under my feet.' "

TO CHRIST.

When I see thee hanging, bleeding,
Dying, on the cruel tree.
Pale in woe, yet interceding
For the men that murdered thee;
How can I refrain from giving
Life and soul and all away,
On thy promise ever living.
Thee adoring night and day!

When I see thee upward breaking
From the grave, on high to stand,
And thy rightful empire taking
At the Father's blest right hand;
Can I longer doubt thy favor,
Or thy willingness to bless?
No, my interceding Saviour,
Words can ne'er my hope express.

When I feel the fresh bedewing
Of thy spirit on my heart,
All the Father's mercy viewing,
In the gifts thy pangs impart;
Faith accepts the heavenly sealing
Tenderness and joy combine,
Peace o'er all my soul is stealing,
I am Christ's, and Christ is mine!

Thus, when life's short day is ending,
And this mortal yields its power,
May thy Spirit condescending
Cleanse and arm me for the hour!
At the river's brink arriving,
In thy smile I lose my fear,
Victory then crowns my striving.
Death is gain, for Christ is here!

GOD BE MERCIFUL TO ME A SINNER!

Several comments may be made on this familiar prayer.

I. *It is a* SINNER'S PRAYER. If the Bible gave us the prayers only of great saints, we might be at a loss; it gives us the prayers of great sinners. This man is a Publican; and a Publican is *prima-facie* a sinner. Our Lord evidently means it to be so understood.

The proper place for the sinner is the place of prayer. The very best thing a Publican can do is to go direct to God in prayer. Thus the sinful Zaccheus placed himself in the way. He was perhaps a laughing-stock in that tree by the wayside; but he knew every thing depended on his seeing Christ. It is a blessed thing for a *sinner* to have words put into his mouth with which to go to God. If the worst malefactor living could come to the point of turning, here are the words with which to turn.

There was a horrible wretch suspended on the cross at Golgotha; in his agonies he resolved to pray. He saw dying beside him the Saviour of the world. He poured out his sinful, breaking, expiring soul in one great but short petition: "Lord, remember me!" and in a few moments he was in the arms of that Lord in Paradise. What a blessed cheering lesson, that sinners may pray!

II. *It is a* SIMPLE PRAYER. It is very short; far shorter than the Pharisee's, though his was short for a Pharisee. Perhaps we have not all he said, in amplification of his righteousness. This has but a single petition. There is no multiplication of request. When a man goes to God in earnest, he will usually dwell on the *one thing* which is his burden; this will swell within him — this will overflow — this will break into language. There have been times, O reader! when all our wishes seemed condensed into one, and we could ask of God only that one thing. Such prayers go from the heart. Infinitely better are they than whole inventories of vain, heartless requests. The message of the heart — that is what God looks at; what the soul pants, wrestles, and longs for, can not live without, yea, almost *dies* for; this is the prayer God hears. As a man prays, when all is at stake — when a firstborn is at the brink of the pit — when he is in extreme peril — as you will pray when God shall stand over you, saying, "Thou shalt die and not live!" This is praying in earnest, and it is always simple. *All great things are simple.* Mighty heavings of desire break away over conventional forms. Like Paul he could say, "One thing I do;" one thing I want. He summoned all his powers to give impetus to one vast petition; it was for a simple good, and that good was, *Mercy.*

"Mercy, good Lord, mercy I crave,
This is the total sum:
For mercy, Lord, is all my suit,
Lord, let thy mercy come!"

(STERNHOLD.)

III. It is a LOWLY PRAYER. Every thing in his posture and carriage evinces this; but the words still more. He gives himself one title only, and that the lowest, "*a sinner.*" Has he heard what the Pharisee has just been saying of him to God? Ah! he cares not. God, he knows full well, needs not the information; nay, he needs it not himself. Others can not think worse of him than he thinks of himself. The sense of God's all seeing eye, as upon us, and of his spotless holiness as against us, makes the judgment by men of very little value. It is then a small thing to be judged by man's judgment. This is the true source of humility. Looking at ourselves as God looks at us tends to cut down our high thoughts. "Pride was not made for man." It is abomination to God. Above all, spiritual pride is an inward sin of a deep dye; because it is a vaunting of ourselves in that which, if indeed possessed, we have received as beggars from the hand of God. And pride on our knees, self-complacency in sackcloth, conceit of our own goodness in prayer — what are these but so many insults to Jehovah! "The rich hath He sent empty away." These boasters, and carnal self-pleasers are they, whom infinite purity and holiness loves to crush. For see the moral of the parable, (v. 14,) "For every one that exalteth himself shall be abased." How often is it said! how constantly do we need the repetition! Perhaps the very man who is now saying, "*I* need it not," needs it most. (Matt. 23: 12,) " Whosoever shall exalt himself shall be abased." (James 4: 6,) "God resisteth the proud, but giveth grace unto the humble." We must come in prayer, as the culprit comes, as the leper comes, "or even as this publican."

IV. *It is a* PENITENT PRAYER. This above all things it is. The voice of true compunction breaks through, as in a sob of grief. A sinner! a sinner I just as the leper, under the law, was to stand afar, and cry: "Unclean! unclean." O ye hardened sinners; ye unhumbled Pharisees; how little do ye know of the grief of a soul pouring itself out to God under a sense of the turpitude, magnitude and multitude of sins! To you, how much of the prayers of the church, and of the prayers of David, must be a dead letter ! How little conception have ye of the solitary moanings of one who loathes himself on account of sin, and smites his breast on account of his impotency, and acknowledges his utter vileness and unworthiness! God's law laid closely to the conscience, and God's holiness beaming on the sinful heart, work such a contrast and conflict that the best expression is often that of Job: "I abhor myself and repent in dust and ashes." And though you now think this whole matter an exaggeration, and flatter yourself in your own eyes until your iniquity be found hateful, it is because your eyes have never been opened, and "ye must be born again!" In the hour of true repentance, there is such a justifying of God and such a condemning of self as sometimes dissolves the soul into a penitential sorrow which bedews and kisses the feet of Christ; which will not forgive itself even when He forgives; which exclaims, "To *me* who am less than the least of all saints" — to me "the chief of sinners." Nay, what can be more full of pathos, than this gush of heart from the convinced Publican: "God be merciful to me a sinner!"

V. *It is a* PRAYER OF FAITH. This we might argue from the effect. Without faith it is impossible to please him: but this *did* please him. He that cometh to God must believe that he is, and that he is a rewarder of them who diligently seek him. The Publican so believed, and so came, and so sought, and was so rewarded. He that is in need is to ask of God; "but let him ask in faith," says the Apostle James. Many a man has had a deep, and despairing, and almost damning sense of his guilt, so as to be driven to the cries of Cain and the suicide of Judas, and yet has never uttered this prayer; for this reason, that he has had no belief in God as a justifier of the ungodly, and no sight of Christ as a sufficient and willing Saviour. It is a lesson we are slow to learn, yet most true and important, that true sorrow for sin never begins till there is some sight of grace. The Law, in its manifold agency of alarm, conviction, remorse, fear, horror, crushing of soul, can only harden. Increase this, until it reach utter despondency, like that of the lost, who have legal awakening in its extreme, still it has no tincture of gracious affection. But let the *Cross* appear; let God be revealed as ready to pardon; let the gift of his Son attract the love of the heart; let the blood of Calvary trickle warmly over the obdurate bosom; and these morose, proud, and relentless habits give place to childlike sorrow and melting contrition. Then the soul can *pray*. "Behold he prayeth!" Then the sinner can pray to *God*, as no longer vengeful and unforgiving; and can call on him by his chosen name, "The Lord, the Lord God merciful and gracious." Then he can utter the petition which Christ has honored, "God be merciful to me a sinner!"

VI. *It is an* ACCEPTED PRAYER. Often, alas! we pray, and never afterward concern ourselves, as to whether we have been heard or not. The Pharisee is so sure of his own merits that he scarcely needs to ask. The Publican, whether he knows it or not, is heard and answered: "I tell you, this man went down to his house justified rather than the other." Reader, it is a blessed thing to go from the sanctuary to the home, with a justified soul: many have so gone; and you might so go. The whole need not a physician; the Pharisee sought no pardon; but they that are sick —the Publican — the sinner — such as you and I, make this the burden of prayer, and earnestly beseech God to show us this favor. Could you, as you now read, under a pressing, poignant sense of your own unworthiness, and transgression, and defilement, abandon all your good works, good intentions, and good feelings; and as a sinner, empty of all good, of all power, and of all preparation, could you, just as you are, look away from that dark chaos within you, on which you have been gazing, to the Lamb of God who taketh away the sin of the world; could you be all on a sudden withdrawn from looking self- ward to looking *Christ*-ward, so as to be absorbed in the contemplation of an excellency, a love, a mercy, a grace, a forgiveness, which ask no condition, and brook no bounds; and could you, in all your present sense of hardness, impenitency, and unpreparedness, flee forever from all your own deservings, and your own strivings, and cast yourself headlong into the ocean of divine love in Jesus Christ, crying, God be merciful to me a sinner! you would go down to your house *justified*. And how great a blessing would this be! for I have further to say of this petition.

VII. *It is the* PRAYER OF A SAVED SOUL. Has it not been heard? Has it not been answered? Has not Christ spoken the whole parable to teach this very thing? Has not the Publican gone down to his house justified? Has not God been merciful to him a sinner? Then of a truth he is forever saved! His sins, which were many, are forgiven, and he loves much and goes on his way rejoicing. Can any thing be more just cause of joy to a human soul than a consciousness of pardon and divine acceptance? It is salvation begun. The assurance may not ensue upon the prayer. One may be in darkness and yet be a true believer. Those are not the safest Christians who boast of the most unchanging frames. Their comparisons of themselves with weaker brethren savor of the Pharisee's gratulations. But the soul is safe, which has even once fled for refuge to lay hold on the hope set before it in the Gospel. Being joined to Christ it can not be disjoined. It is as pure from guilt as the blood of Christ can wash it. It is as righteous in the sight of law, as the righteousness of Christ can make it. He that spared not his own Son, can not withhold lesser gifts. "Whom he called, them he also justified; and whom he justified, them he also glorified." To be justified, then, is to be saved. This must be admitted, unless you can produce some power able to effect a separation between the Head and the members: and what power shall this be? Tribulation, distress, persecution, famine, peril, sword, death, life, angels, principalities, powers, things present, things to come, height, depth, any other creature? nay, in all these things we are more than conquerors, through him that loved us!

PAUL GERHARDT'S HYMN

O sacred Head! now wounded,
With grief and shame weighed down;
Now scornfully surrounded
With thorns, thy only crown;
O sacred Head! what glory.
What bliss till now was thine!
Yet, though despised and gory,
I joy to call thee mine.

O noblest brow, and dearest!
In other days the world
All feared when thou appearedst;
What shame on Thee is hurled!
How art thou pale with anguish.
With sore abuse and scorn;
How does that bosom languish
Which once was bright as morn.

The blushes late residing
Upon that holy cheek,
The roses once abiding
Upon those lips so meek;
Alas! they have departed;
Wan Death has rifled all!
For, weak and broken-hearted,
I see thy body fall.

What thou, my Lord, hast suffered
  Was all for sinners' gain;
Mine, mine was the transgression,
  But thine the deadly pain.
Lo! here I fall, my Saviour!
  'Tis I deserve thy place.
Look on me with thy favor,
  Vouchsafe to me thy grace.

Receive me, my Redeemer,
  My Shepherd, make me thine;
Of every good the fountain.
  Thou art the spring of mine.
Thy lips with love distilling
  And milk of truth sincere.
With heaven's bliss are filling
  The soul that trembles here.

Beside thee. Lord, I've taken
  My place — forbid me not!
Hence will I ne'er be shaken,
  Though thou to death be brought.
If pain's last paleness hold thee,
  In agony opprest —
Then, then will I enfold thee
  Within this arm and breast.

The joy can ne'er be spoken,
  Above all joys beside,
When in thy body broken
  I thus with safety hide.

My Lord of life, desiring
 Thy glory now to see.
Beside the cross expiring
 I'd breathe my soul to thee.

What language shall I borrow
 To thank thee, dearest Friend,
For this, thy dying sorrow,
 Thy pity without end!
O make me thine forever!
 And should I fainting be,
Lord, let me never, never
 Outlive my love to Thee,

Be near when I am dying,
 Show thy cross to me!
And for my succor flying,
 Come, Lord, to set me free.
These eyes new faith receiving,
 From Jesus shall not move,
For he who dies believing,
 Dies safely through thy love.

Note. — The author of this translation, from Paul Gerhardt, desires to say that it has been frequently republished with changes and mutilations, which do great injustice to the German original. — A.

OH! FOR MORE FEELING!

What language is more common among awakened sinners than this: "I can not feel that I am a sinner. And yet I know that I have broken God's holy law. I acknowledge that I am justly condemned. I am deeply distressed at times with the thought that I must surely perish. But my great burden is that I can not feel this. I have no deep sense of my own sinfulness. My constant and agonizing prayer has been for months, 'Lord! break this hard unfeeling heart!'"

There are unhappy souls, we must admit, whom God has deserted, who do not and can not feel their lost condition; and who are designated by the Apostle as "past feeling." Do you, afflicted reader, class yourself among these? You know that you can not. You are in distress; and what distresses you? That you are calm and unmoved in the midst of your sins? That the awful position of your soul is unnoticed by you? That you have no desire to return to God?

"No, this is not my condition," you instantly answer. "I do feel; yet it is not because I am a sinner, but because my heart is so hard and unfeeling."

Now suppose you transfer this experience from your soul to your body, and see how unfounded are your troubles. You are afflicted with a deep-seated malady; it is invisible, it gives no pain; and yet its effects are apparent, in the wasting of your body. Suppose you were to argue thus: "I know that there is a deadly disease preying upon my vitals, and I desire to be cured; but I feel no pain — I do not see the loathsome seat of evil. If I could only feel and see this, I would call for the physician."

You do know that the disease is there, and you do know that you are a sinner. The Spirit and the law of God have been working this conviction, and your deceitful heart is only shrinking into this refuge of lies in order to delay its flight to the city of refuge.[102]

The word of God gives us no intimation as to the precise amount of feeling which we are to have before we approach Christ for healing. Bartimeus knew that he was blind. This was enough to lead him to the wayside, where Jesus was to pass. There is no evidence that he thought of searching into the nature or origin of his blindness. He knew that he was blind, and that was enough to force from him the cry, "Jesus, thou Son of David, have mercy on me!" The Israelites, who were bitten by the fiery serpents, were not required to trace the effects of the subtle poison as it entered the circulation, or to mark the symptoms of its deadly progress, before they looked at the brazen serpent for healing. The moment they felt the venomous fang they might look and be healed. Since it was so with the types of the sinner and the cross, is it not equally so with the antitypes?

Where has God said, Produce so much conviction, feel so and so, in regard to your sin, humble your soul to that particular point of anguish and grief, and then you may have Christ and his free grace? Nay; on such a plan no inquiring soul could ever know his warrant to believe, because he could never ascertain whether his conviction, grief, and anguish were enough.

"Let not conscience make you linger;
Nor of fitness fondly dream:
All the fitness he requireth
Is to feel your need of him."

It was truly said by President Edwards, "that those who are partly convinced of sin are not apt to think themselves greatly convinced; and the reason is this: men judge of the degree of their own convictions of sin by two things jointly considered, namely, the degree of sense which they have of guilt and pollution, and the degree of cause they have for such a sense, in the degree of their real sinfulness. It is really no argument of any great conviction of sin for some men to think themselves to be very sinful, beyond most others in the world; because they are so indeed very plainly and notoriously. And therefore a far less conviction of sin may incline such a one to think so than another; he must be very blind indeed, not to be sensible of it. But he that is truly under great conviction of sin, naturally thinks this to be his case. It appears to him that the cause he has to be sensible of guilt and pollution is greater than others have, and therefore he ascribes his sensibleness of this to the greatness of his sin, and not to the greatness of his sensibility."

This difficulty as to a want of feeling arises wholly from a wrong view of what salvation is. We fail to see in it a perfect gratuity to sinners. To *sinners* I say, for the whole effort of the soul, in all its struggles, is to make some preparation, to be in some peculiar state of mind, before it can receive the free gift. But Christ came to call not the righteous, but sinners; the invitations of the Gospel are to SINNERS. No one, indeed, will come to the physician who has not a sense of want; but there is no merit, nor any proper preparation, in such sense of want. It is only hungering and thirsting. If you hunger after salvation, come; if you are athirst, come; if you are heavy laden because you can not feel your sins, *come*.

Let us, however, suppose this difficulty to be removed. You are satisfied that certain convictions of sin are not prescribed as necessary to your acceptance of Christ. Satan and your own deceitful heart have not yet exhausted their subterfuges. You now are troubled because you feel no love, nor joy; and the soul often complains that it has even no desire for salvation. It seems to be your determined purpose to obstruct the way by every possible impediment. Can you conceive of a drowning man refusing to seize the rope which is thrown to him, because he doubts whether he feels gratitude enough to the friend who has thrown it; or because he is not certain whether he rightly wishes to be saved? Surely Satan has blinded the minds of them that believe not, when he can thus prevent them from simply accepting eternal life.

There are two grand errors upon which all these difficulties of the inquiring soul rest. The first is that there is some work, preparation, or experience demanded previous to a surrender of the heart to Christ. The second is, that salvation is an emotion, or a feeling, or a series of these, instead of a new life begun in faith. All the thoughts, emotions, or acts of the soul, before it rests upon Christ, are utterly worthless in the sight of God. "LORD, I BELIEVE," is the first utterance of the new-born soul. Preceding exercises, if they have any value, only lead the soul to this confession, and then the feelings are the fruits of that new life derived at the cross.

You may have been weeks or months waiting for these feelings to come — wrestling with God in prayer that he would send them — and deeply disturbed because the prayer was not answered. Did you ever go to the Word of God, and put your finger upon the command that you must have this feeling or that feeling, before you could believe on Christ? Did our Lord tell Nicodemus to go home and wait until his heart was broken, and then come again and receive life? No, He told him to believe. Did the apostles tell the thousands who were awakened by Peter's sermon on the day of Pentecost, to wait for farther light or further conviction? No, the command was, repent. It was an act to be performed then; and among the three thousand who did receive Christ there, must there not have been an infinite variety of experience? Some felt as you feel — perhaps some delayed as you delay — but the three thousand, without waiting, received the proffered salvation. Did Paul advise the trembling jailer to wait until he was better prepared to come? No, but out of the very jaws of suicide to believe in that Saviour who received him. A young man came to the writer of these pages a few weeks ago under great concern, asking what he must do to be saved. He was directed to the Cross and its Divine Victim, and to a simple receiving of the Lord Jesus Christ as the only Way of life. A few days after he came rejoicing in hope, saying: "I did not know how easy a thing conversion was. I thought there would be some great and wonderful change in my feelings before I came to the Cross." This is but the old story of Naaman, or rather of the human heart, refusing to receive a free salvation; looking at its own corruptions and its amendment, instead of the great object of faith which is so prominently set before us in the Word of God.

Let the reader look at the sum of these errors and disheartening delays. *You are unwilling to be saved by grace.* You do not confess it, but your posture proves it; you are waiting, waiting, waiting, months or even years, to be borne away into some griefs or raptures, which, it may be, God has no purpose of bestowing upon you. The effect is preposterously put before the cause, feeling before faith. If you could only feel hope, grief, terror, love, you would believe. God's declaration of mercy would then be true to you. Ah! sinner, it is true to you now, whether you feel or not. Feeling becomes self-righteousness, if it takes the place of the righteousness of Christ. "Would you feel now? Only believe. It is at the Cross (that is, believing) that the burden falls from the back, and tears of genuine feeling from the eyes.

The Lord will happiness divine
On contrite hearts bestow;
Then tell me, gracious God, is mine
A contrite heart or no?

I hear, but seem to hear in vain,
Insensible as steel;
If aught is felt, 'tis only pain
To find I can not feel

I sometimes think myself inclined
To love thee if I could;
But often feel another mind
Averse to all that's good.

My best desires are faint and few —
I fain would strive for more;
But when I cry, "My strength renew,"
Seem weaker than before.

Thy saints are comforted, I know,
And love thy house of prayer;
I therefore go where others go,
But find no comfort there.

Oh! make this heart rejoice or ache,
Decide this doubt for me;
And if it be not broken, break,
And heal it if it be.

HAVE I COME TO CHRIST?

There is nothing which should awaken surprise in the statement, that believers bear certain marks by which they may discover themselves to be such; for religion works a real and important change, which admits of being ascertained. Many are the treatises which have been written on this subject, and it would be easy to add to their number, because every fruit of grace might in a sense be called an evidence, and the recital of all these would fill a volume. It is not intended now to enter upon so large a field, nor to treat the whole round of Christian evidences. It will be more expedient to contemplate the subject only as it stands related to our proper topic; in other words, to examine the evidences of a gracious state under this single aspect, as evidences of *having come to Christ.*

Before proceeding to indicate any marks of faith, it will be desirable to state a few principles, the neglect of which has given rise much confusion; these principles have a direct bearing on all that is to be said in the sequel.

The evidences which are to to be proposed are not for the world, but for the inquirer. On the world there can be no marks but those of external conduct, and these are often fallacious. He who would know his own state must go deeper than this; for as the venerable Stoddard observes: "All visible signs are common to converted and unconverted men; and a relation of experiences among the rest." Not only the world, but the most pious and experienced church officers may be deceived, and take chaff for wheat;

the sincere believer will therefore aim to push his search more to the root of things.

These marks must be of divine authority. Hundreds of rules have been laid down, and pressed with great earnestness, which have nevertheless no foundation in the Word of God, but are barely the inventions of men, sometimes of imprudent and erroneous men. In times of unusual awakening, and times when there is earnestness for particular doctrines, it is common for many new tests to be proposed. Thus, for example, the day has been when a man would not be reckoned a true Christian, unless lie abandoned all his goods; or unless he was fully prepared for martyrdom; or unless he was delivered from all self-love; or unless he was willing to be damned; or unless he professed full assurance of hope; or unless he had attained sinless perfection. By setting up such tests, weak and trembling believers have often been cast into needless despondency, while presumptuous zealots have triumphed. No discrimination has the slightest value here which is not founded on clear declarations of the Scripture; and these are so abundant as to cut off every pretext of arrogant inventors. "To the Law and to the Testimony."

The marks of Christian character go together, as parts of an undivided whole. There is such a unity and symmetry in the religious life, as proceeding from " one and the selfsame Spirit," that we can no more have a half-Christianity than a half-life. For, first, since there is a total depravity in the unrenewed, and since there is no grace, even apparently the smallest, which is not the fruit of regeneration, it follows, *that any one undeniable evidence would ascertain a soul to be renewed.* If, for example, any one could be absolutely certain of his having genuine faith, or holy love, or gospel humility, he would need to look no further. Just as in a case of suspended animation, when anxious friends surround the body, not knowing but that it is a corpse; there are many signs of animal life, but one breath, or one opening of the eyes, or one voluntary motion settles the question. But lest this should render any presumptuous, let it be added, that for the same reason, secondly, *the total absence of any one essential mark would ascertain the soul to he unrenewed.* All graces do not indeed blossom and bear at once; there are seasons for particular exercises, and stages in Christian growth; so that this rule is not to be hastily applied. But of its general truth no one can be in doubt, who will reflect, that the absolute and undeniable want of humility, or of brotherly kindness, if it could be ascertained, would as certainly stamp a man an enemy of God, as perjury or murder. In a word, the Christian life, though not always acting in the same manner, or the same degree, is always fully present in renewed minds.

It is the reality, and not the degree, of these evidences, which is the present object of our search. In another connection we ought to be deeply concerned about the small measure of our piety, and ought daily and with tears to strive for its highest degrees; but when the inquiry is whether we have any piety whatever, it is not a question of degree; and many a humble soul needs the suggestion. There maybe life where there is little strength and little development. The new-born child is as truly alive as the giant. This should not make us willing to remain children, but it should keep us from pronouncing that there is no renewal, because its evidences are small in degree. At the same time it is to be acknowledged, that the principal reason why any real Christians are in doubt as to their acceptance, is that the degree of their evidence is so small; the fire burns so low that it can not be perceived among the ashes; and the obvious method for such persons is to desist from the search for that which is so small, and to strive that it may become greater.

The evidence of our conversion is not he sought in any one moment, hut in the whole tenor of the life. Regeneration itself indeed is not gradual; the transition from death to life is instantaneous; but we are not competent to judge of that single instant. Too great stress has undoubtedly been laid on the marked character of the first exercises supposed to be saving; and the error has operated in twofold evil, by darkening the views of the desponding, and making the self-deceiver more presumptuous. It is not by any single moment, even though it were the best, that we can judge of the genuineness of piety. Judged thus, the stony ground hearers, believing and rejoicing, Matt. 13:20, would have been unblamable. In applying tests, we must look at tendencies as well as frames and states, and must consider the constancy no less than the ardor of feelings and acts. Take into view the whole of your religious life for years, if you would arrive at a sound conclusion.

The last of these preliminaries is not the least important; it is, that *the difficulty lies, not so much in laying down marks, as in discovering their existence in the soul.* Marks there are, and those infallible, as founded on clear Scriptures, which are nevertheless obscure in some true believers, and seemingly present in some hypocrites. It would be a sad mistake to come with any formula, expecting to apply it as one does a chemical test for the discovery of a given ingredient in a mixture. The best treatises may be abused in this way. We may say with truth, for example, that true religion proceeds from the Holy Spirit; is accompanied with spiritual views and relish, and supreme love to God; but the problem is to ascertain the existence of these very marks. Still it is important to have in the mind a few unquestionable tokens of the new nature; if for no other reason, that we may be always trying to realize them in our experience.

Since the question is, whether we have come to Christ

or not, it may serve a useful purpose to recur in thought to the time when it was possible to come to Christ by a bodily approach, that is, the days of his ministry. In those days he often uttered the words of invitation, such as, "Come unto me," "Follow me;" and these in the first instance were obeyed literally. Many came to him, and remained with him. This, their external coming, was only in order to a more important and spiritual coming, by means of faith; but one throws light upon the other. Those who so came to Christ forsook all their previous associations; they henceforth were present with him; they were found in possession of those things for which they so came; and they stood in new relations to Christ and to his people. In all these respects their case may guide in the inquiry how any soul in our day may be known to have come to Christ. Disavowing, as above, any attempt to exhaust this subject, let me point out a few evidences of this great change.

I. *He who has come to Christ has forsaken his former associations.* When Jesus called disciples on the sea of Tiberias, he said, "Come ye after me;" upon which Simeon and Andrew straightway "forsook their nets and followed him." James and John "left their . . . . . father und went after him."(Mark 1:16-20.) In reference to which, one of the persons here named, said afterwards: "Lo, we have left all, and have followed thee." (Mark 10:28.) That coming to Christ involves the abandoning of what comes into rivalry with him, is apparent from his own words in Luke 14:33: "Whosoever he be of you that forsaketh not all that he hath, he can not be my disciple." And when an inquirer pleaded that he must first attend to the funeral of his father, "Jesus said unto him, Follow me; and let the dead bury their dead." (Matt. 8:22.) This separation from former ties is represented as a death, nay, as a crucifixion: "The world is crucified unto me, and I unto the world." (Gal. 6:14.) It is a divorce from the law, as to its curse and penalty and slavish fear: " Wherefore, my brethren, ye also are become dead to the law, by the body of Christ." (Rom. 7:4.) It is no less a divorce from sin: "they that are Christ's, have crucified the flesh, with the affections and lusts." (Gal. 4:24.) That which is to be forsaken for Christ's sake, might all be summed up in this particular, it is sin. When we renounce, the world, the flesh, and the devil, and the pomps and vanities of the world, it is really the sin that is in these things which we renounce. The very intent of Christ's coming was, "that he might destroy the works of the devil;" and those who come to Christ have ceased from these works. The gift of the Holy Spirit has for its object the renewal of the soul in holiness; or, what is the same thing, its restitution to spiritual health. Religion is only another name for the normal condition of the soul, and in its complete state the balance and perfection of all the faculties. For this cause it is that sanctification becomes evidence of justification. Sin can not reign in a renewed soul. The believer makes great use of this in judging of his state. He hates those things which he once loved. The empty pleasures of the world, forbidden indulgences, sensual joys, unrighteous gains, every form of falsehood, deception, selfishness, pride, malice, revenge, and whatsoever God condemns, have become as odious to him as some of them may once have been delightful.

The question is then appropriate: *What have you forsaken?* Sins will exist, and may for a time prevail, in truly regenerate persons, "for there is no man that sinneth not;" but they are objects of abhorrence, and do not indicate the character. The seventh chapter of the Epistle to the Romans merits close study in this connection; for it records the experience of a renewed soul, yet of one who cried, as the reader may possibly have done: "0 wretched man that I am! who shall deliver me from the body of this death?" (v. 24.) Yet this regenerate soul could also say, in regard to this very sin, and in terms which no ungodly man could adopt: "That which I do I allow not; for what I would that do I not; but what I hate that do I;" "To will is present with me;" "The evil that I would not, that I do;" "For I delight in the law of God, after the inward man." As to the abiding temper of his mind, the true Christian has abandoned his ancient country, and entered on a new. The tide in his affections, under some temporary influence may run the wrong way, but the main stream still flows away from sin.

If then you would judge of your state, ask how you are affected towards the things which you profess to have left for Christ. Have you bidden farewell to sin? Do you hate it? Do you loathe it? Your past sins; are they still bitter and humbling, so that you are made to possess the iniquities of your youth? Your present sins; into which you have been plunged, as if in spite of yourself; do you groan under them, as within the coils of a serpent? Your future sins; is the thought of yet further offending Christ horrible to you? Have you abandoned the world? Do you shun the road to sin, by avoiding and deprecating temptation? Are you endeavoring to mortify sin, and has God granted you some success in the work? These questions, and such as these, may properly be suggested to those who persuade themselves that they have become disciples. And if it truly appear that in these respects old things have passed away, there will be good reason to believe that all things have become new.

II. *He who has come to Christ is actually with Christ.* Does not all personal coming imply this? He is brought into the presence of Christ; or to vary the expression, Christ is present to him. This includes several particulars, which may be noticed with profit.

1. *Believing makes Christ present.* We have already seen that this is the very essence of coming to Christ: it is by believing that we come: "Faith is the evidence (the *elenchus* or conviction) of things not seen." (Heb. 11:1.)

Nature would prompt the wish that we had lived in the days of Christ's bodily presence on earth, but faith reveals a Saviour "whom having not seen ye love, in whom though now ye see him not, yet *believing*, ye rejoice, with joy unspeakable and full of glory," He is the same to faith, in heaven and on earth, "Jesus Christ, the same yester-day, to-day and forever." Now is Christ present to your apprehension? Have you come to him in this sense? As the question is concerning your own mental state, you may fairly appeal to consciousness; do you then believe? Has the Lord Jesus become to you such an actuality, that your soul has come to deal with him personally, individually, and really, as though he were beside you in bodily presence, and as if his sacred hand was locked in yours? Are you conscious of being near to Christ, and present with him, in such a sense, as to rely on him habitually, yea, this very moment, with all the might of your soul, so that if you were to miss him, or even suspect his absence, you would feel that all the prop of your salvation was gone? The question as to faith is best answered by essaying the acts of faith, that is, by looking at the great object of faith. The best way of removing all dubiety as to whether you have come to Christ, is to come now. And doubtless much of the time which we exhaust in searching for evidence of faith would be better spent by actually believing.

2. *Union makes Christ present.* Nothing can be more truly with us, than that which is one with us. Faith is the bond which unites us to Christ, and thus compacts us into the glorious body of which he is the head. So far as this is a divine transaction, beyond the sphere of experience, it is too transcendent for our cognizance, and can not be summoned as evidence; but this union has its visible fruits, and it is these, after which we must inquire. These fruits coincide with justification, adoption, and sanctification, and may be treated of under the following head:

3. *He who is with Christ has communion with him.* Those who hearkened to his voice and came to him, when he was on earth, enjoyed converse with him, and delighted in his society; in the days of rejoicing, when the "children of the bride-chamber" were too happy to fast.

Nor are such condescensions altogether wanting now. He still knocks at the door, and to him who hears and opens, he comes in and sups. Our views are habitually too low, in regard to the possibility of enjoying Christ's presence on earth. It is to be the joy of our heaven hereafter, but God pours out to us some prelibations on earth. The reality of spiritual enjoyment, where the soul goes forth to Christ in his holy spiritual attributes, affords bright evidence of having really come to him. Ask the question of your closet, your church, and your sacraments.

III. *He who has come to Christ has some possession of that for which he came.* For what did you come to Christ? The answer is easy, for SALVATION. It is too common to speak of salvation as a remote or even a contingent blessing. *The believer is already saved.* His sins are pardoned. He can never come into condemnation. He is united to Christ, and nothing can separate him from God's love. He has a new life, and a new nature, being regenerated and restored to God's image, and conformed by sanctification to his nature. He has the peace of God begun in his soul. In these brief but comprehensive statements, which none can deny, is included salvation; and it is for this that the soul comes to Christ.

All this is admitted and incontestable; but the difficulty is to derive from these truths such practical marks as shall enable us to try our own state. As to pardon, it is the very thing of which we desire to be assured; it can not, therefore, be the medium of proof. This is true, yet pardon is coordinate with some other blessings for which we approach the Lord, and which are cognizable in our experience. Two of these shall be mentioned.

1. *The filial disposition.* He who comes to Christ for pardon, and obtains it, receives a salutation like that in Luke 7:48: "Thy sins are forgiven." Faith and justification are followed by peace, (Rom. 5:1,) as is abundantly shown in those glowing chapters. Were there more of simple affiance in the word of promise, there would be more of this evidence of having obtained pardon. Though, like the "white stone," it is incommunicable to man, I am disposed to believe it is in the most rejoicing Christians the chief ground of their comfortable persuasion that God is reconciled. They feel him to be so. His love (to them) is shed abroad in their hearts, and they cry Abba, Father. Examine, my reader, whether this be in you and abound. Is the spirit of servility and fear cast out? Is the blood of Christ so sprinkled on your heart and conscience as to purge it from dead works, and release it from a sense of wrath? When you kneel in prayer, is there any flowing of the affections in a deep channel towards God, as a beloved Father in heaven? Unless you mistake here, there is reason to trust, if such are your exercises, that your pardon has been sealed. But the obscurity of single evidences makes it desirable to gain the confirmation of concurrent tokens; hence remember that

2. *Holiness* is a part of salvation, and a principal blessing for which believers come to Christ. The subject is too wide to be discussed in a paragraph. Its difficulties however are not theological but practical. All agree that sanctification is good proof of justification; but am I sanctified? Here is the critical question, into which, indeed, all the others might be resolved. As long as we live we ought to be daily pressing this inquiry, whether we are growing in conformity to God.

Under this head, the subject of sanctification may be viewed in another aspect. *He who has come to Christ resembles Christ.* The principle is obvious. Now holiness is resemblance to Christ. If the Christian graces and fruits of the Spirit are found in us, they show that we have been with Christ, and have caught some traits of his character. The subject is vast, so as not to allow details. There is not a virtue, grace, habit, act, feeling, thought, enjoined or approved in Scripture, which may not come in for a share in this examination; and hence the topic must be dismissed with a simple recommendation to practice.

3. *Peace* — beautiful, heavenly word — is a part of salvation; it has already gained our attention. In quest of peace we ventured to seek Christ, even before we had a spiritual relish for holiness, and he graciously vouchsafed not to cast us off for preferring the effect to the cause. But true peace is a divine quality, and where it prevails shows that the soul has been brought to Christ. There is a false peace, and the chief task is to distinguish this. Recourse must be had to the characters of true peace, which have been frequently indicated; the chief of these being that genuine peace is founded on Christ, is consistent with high activity, is inseparable from earnest endeavors to maintain universal holiness. If the tranquility which followed your supposed believing has left you easy in conscience and less scrupulous about offending; if you have less veneration of God's majesty, and less fear of offending, and less sense of your need of attoning blood, and less hatred of corrupt habits and motions, then be assured it is a spurious, and is likely to be a destructive calm. But if in connection with a persuasion of pardon, and an increasing purity, you grow happier and happier, there seems to be ground to think that you are saved; in other words, that you have possession of that for which you sought Christ.

IV. *He who has come to Christ stands in new relations to Christ and to his people:* and of this he has some inward feeling, which enables him to use it as a testimony.

1. *A relation of friendship.* Those who companied with Jesus as disciples were his friends, and as such they loved him. To be without this affection is to be under the curse: "If any man love not the Lord Jesus Christ, let him be Anathema Maranatha." If you could only ascertain beyond a doubt that you love the Lord, you would at once possess the highest evidence of faith, and, so far as this inquiry is concerned, might desist from seeking other testimony. Here we are authorized to inquire of our own consciousness, by the example of the Lord Jesus himself, who thrice said to Peter, after his denial: "Simon, son of Jonas, lovest thou me?" And this instance shows us that even an imperfect disciple may sometimes have such witness as to exclaim with a burst of humble, affectionate confidence: "Lord, thou knowest all things; thou knowest that I love thee!" Though the great criterion of love is its fruit, we are not to despise its actual motions in the soul. As no man can be the subject of a high affection without some knowledge of it, we may justly expect to have some direct cognizance of strong love to Christ. Those who are so affected towards him, have his sacred person much in their thoughts, and prize all those means, such as meditation, prayer, and sacraments, which bring him to the thoughts; and have a consciousness of something more than a dull, neutral approbation and respect, being drawn out towards his adorable character and person with a tenderness and warmth as real and unmistakable as what they experience towards friends or offspring. Friends think much of one another; deliberately call up the beloved image; seek correspondence and mutual tokens and messages; ardently press towards society and intimate fellowship; lament over absence; seek the honor and advantage of one another; and ascribe to the most indifferent objects a preciousness if they stand related to the cherished object. Let each of the tests here condensed into a sentence, be

expanded in the secret examination of your heart.

2. *The relation of service.* "If ye love me, keep my commandments." There is no love which does not work obedience. No labor, sacrifice, or suffering is too great for love; thus it fulfills the law. The "love of Christ," says Paul, "constrains us." The whole Christian service of the Church is only love in act. "In this the children of God are manifest, and the children of the devil; whosoever doeth not righteousness is not of God." (John 3:10.) The principle is plain and too familiar to need a word more, but its application demands unremitting care. Look inward on your heart and, backward on your life, and see whether love has wrought performance. "My little children, let us not love in word, neither in tongue, but in deed and truth." (1 John 3:18.) The scope of the inquiry is hence as wide as the entire field of divine command and human obedience, and must be dismissed with a recommendation to make scrutiny as to the fact.

3. *Relation of fraternity to those who are Christ's.* Nothing can be more obvious than the operation of the principle. That which draws men to Christ draws them to one another. The Apostle John, who had learnt the nature of love from lying on the bosom of incarnate Love, declares this mark to be infallible: "This is the message that ye heard from the beginning, that we should love one another. We know that we have passed from death unto life, because we love the brethren." (1 John 3:11, 14.) And his argument is that hatred between brothers is hellish: "Whosoever hateth his brother is a murder," and a Cain; (vv.12 and 15.) "If a man say I love God, and hateth his brother, he is a liar. For he that loveth not his brother, whom he hath seen, how can he love God whom he hath not seen?" (1 John 4:20.) Even though treatises upon the evidences of piety may not give prominence to this mark, it occupies a high place in Scripture, and admits of more easy application to our

experience than many others. Are you then in charity with those who profess to be Christ's friends? Do you freely forgive them, even as you look for forgiveness yourself? even to the seventy times seven? Are you not only forgiving, but prompt to be reconciled, and resolute, at every hazard, to remove the scandal of living in alienation? These are among the most ordinary demands of Christianity; we must look further. In respect to those who give evidence of being not only professed but real believers, do you love the image of Christ as reflected in them? Have you so much of the reality of religion as to have risen above the haughty pharisaism of gilded vulgarity, in those who sit down at the Lord's table with a brother to-day, and deem him unworthy of a salutation to-morrow? Have you been long enough with Jesus to have learnt that connection with him is the greatest of distinctions; greater than the difference between one quality of honor and another, or once degree of fortune and another, or one branch of traffic and another, or one profession and another; and that "Christian is the highest style of man" ? If you have not, "Are ye not then partial in yourselves, and are become judges of evil thoughts?" (James 2:4.) The disregard of this duty is perhaps the most prevalent form of unfaithfulness now existing in our churches, especially in commercial cities; nor do I suppose there is an individual among us who is not guilty of it every day. It is offensive to the Lord Jesus, and diametrically opposed to the whole course of his lovely example. It is not patronage, but respectful love, that we demand in the name of Christ for his poor members, forewarning the rich that the day will arrive when lie will say: "Inasmuch as ye did not to one of the least of these, ye did it not to me." (Matt. 25:45.)

MY TEACHER – MY MASTER

After our blessed Saviour had washed his apostles' feet, he uttered this memorable saying: "Ye call me MASTER and LORD; and ye say well, for so I am."[103] All careful students of Scripture know that in this, and many parallel places, the word "Master" is old-English for Teacher; and that the word "Lord" is equivalent to Ruler, Commander, Prince, or Master. Without changing our excellent translation, we may then regard Jesus as saying: "Ye call me Teacher and Master, and ye do well; for so I am." In every revival of religion, in every sound conversion, the repentant soul takes Christ as his Teacher and his Master. Reader, is it so with thee?

At a time when thousands are openly confessing Christ, it is of infinite moment that every one should see to it that he receives the Lord just as he is offered in the Gospel. Do not here mistake the drift of the caution. In order to justification, remission of sins, absolution, or acceptance with God, you receive the Lord Jesus in his character of Substitute, Vicarious Sacrifice, Lamb of God, and Atoning Priest. But Christ is not merely Priest, he is also Prophet and King. Christ means *Anointed;* and there are three anointings; mark them well. The Prophet is anointed, the Priest is anointed, the King is anointed. The Christ whom you have received, at your believing, is all three at once. This is no nice point of the theological schools, but a plain, simple lesson of Scripture. You think yourself converted; do you receive Jesus, saying to him from the heart: "My Teacher, my Master?"

MY TEACHER!

"Mary!" said the risen Lord to his weeping disciple.[104] "She turned herself, and saith unto him, Rabboni, which is to say. Master," (or in the original Greek,) MY Teacher! Have you, O sinful, but hopeful soul! taken this great teacher, as such, to you? Formerly, you were blind. If you have been made to see, it is He who opened your eyes. He is the "true light." Predicted in the Old Testament as the great Prophet of His people, He is the giver of all their spiritual knowledge. Until He touched your eyes, you were in gross darkness as to the very elements of saving truth. This ignorance did not appear so great, till the time when the Law entered your soul and made you tremble. Then, almost wildly, you went to and fro, asking: "Men and brethren, what must I do?" Your former knowledge was now turned into foolishness. You were willing to be taught as a babe. The language of your thoughts was: "Who will tell me the meaning of these mysterious words: 'Repent,' 'Believe,' 'Come to Christ,' 'Look unto Christ,' 'Yield yourselves to God'?" At length you were illuminated, as to the import of these terms, by being made to experience the blessed reality. Old things passed away, all things became new. You learned what repentance is, by repenting; what faith is, by believing; and what coming to Christ is, by casting your guilty soul upon his propitiation. In all this, it was your Prophet who enlightened; and he must enlighten still.

"Never man spake like this man;" so they said during his ministry on earth. His followers were called "disciples," that is, scholars or learners. He was a condescending teacher. "Learn of me, for I am meek and lowly."[105] Tens of thousands were taught by him then; millions have been taught by him since; for his school is open to this day.

Your blessed Teacher, O disciple! instructs by the Spirit and the Word. These two, which God hath joined, let not man put asunder. Seek not light of the Spirit without the Word. Rely not on the letter of the Word without the Spirit.[106] Come to Jesus for both. Though in his humanity Christ is in heaven, he is on earth in his divinity, and by his Spirit; as he promised: "When he, the Spirit of Truth, is come, he will guide you into all truth."[107] Delay not, amidst the excitements of early love, to place yourself at the feet of Jesus, and to learn holy wisdom from his gracious lips.

MY MASTER!

If your supposed turning to God has made you easy in your sins, your conversion is counterfeit. "Why call ye me Lord, Lord, and do not the things which I say?"[108] The very instant that you took Christ for your Redeemer, you took him for your Lord and Master. Faith and Obedience, it is true, are not the same. Faith, and not Obedience, is the instrument of justification.[109] Nevertheless, Faith and Obedience are sisters who always walk hand in hand. When your pained heart, looking to Christ bleeding on the cross, said, My Saviour! it said equally, My Master! This is obedience in the bud. Faith worketh by love, and love realizes itself in obedience.

There is something inexpressibly delightful in exchanging that old legal bondage, under which duties were rendered to an unreconciled God, amidst groans and weakness, for a willing service, a gospel liberty, in which obligation is swallowed up in grateful, admiring acquiescence. Who that beholds, by faith,

the loveliness of such a Lord, can fail to obey him? Precious is the relation to Jesus, by which we receive the law out of his hands. Thus the tables of stone were sacredly laid away under the golden propitiatory![110] "Ye serve the LORD CHRIST."[111] Never can you obey so sweetly as when you render even the smallest service of menial life to him;

as if you said in your heart. Though working late with axe or needle, in factory or kitchen, "I do this for *my Master.*" Is not the very title welcome to thine ear, O converted soul? "Where wouldst thou go to find a better service?

"How sweetly doth My Master sound; my Master!
As ambergris leaves a rich scent
Unto the taster;
So do these words a sweet content,
An oriental fragrancy: my Master!
My Master, shall I speak? Oh! that to Thee,
My servant were a little so,
As flesh may be;
That these two words might creep, and grow
To some degree of spiciness to Thee!
For when My Master (which alone is sweet
And e'en in my unworthiness pleasing)
Shall call and meet
My servant, as Thee not displeasing;
Thy call is but the breathing of the sweet
This breathing would with gains by sweet'ning me,
(As sweet things traffic when they meet,)
Return to Thee;
And so this new commerce and sweet
Should, all my life, employ and busy me."

So sang the holy poet, of whom Izaak Walton writes thus: "He seems to rejoice in the thoughts of that word Jesus, and say that the adding of these words, 'My Master,' to it, and the often repetition of them, seemed to perfume his mind, and leave an oriental fragrancy in his very breath." Distrust that sort of experience, dear reader, which is unaccompanied with a fresher purpose to please Christ. Rejecting, with indignation and loathing, all works of your own, considered as the procuring cause of your justification, at the same time perform all the works you can, as a service of love to Him whom you call Master and Lord.

There are those who dream of being saved in their sins. By a horrible abuse, they talk loudly of being washed in the blood of Christ and placed in gospel liberty, "while they themselves are the servants of corruption."[112]

What is this but to cast defilement over the sacred tree on which the immaculate Jesus died? By this name is he called, because he saves his people *"from their sins."* Though, therefore, you trusted in his righteousness, and not in your own, for acceptance and pardon, you accepted him as your commander and king, to obey him forever. At the blessed moment when you received him as your satisfying Priest and bleeding sacrifice, you uttered with one and the same breath, if we may so speak, the aspiration, "Lord, I give myself to thee to be justified;" and, "Lord, I give myself to thee to be sanctified." I believe — I love! My new life, of trust and obedience, begins here. My Saviour — my Master!

MY TEACHER! MY MASTER!

Let us take them both together, for the Lord Jesus is both. In both characters let us draw nigh to him. We are both ignorant and sinful, and the ignorance and sin act and re-act on each other. The connection between light and love, between truth and holy living, is often set forth in Scripture: "If we say that we have fellowship in him, and walk in darkness, we lie, and do not the truth."[113] Be it our daily business to resort to the Lord Jesus, as a present Saviour, for spiritual instruction and commandments to be obeyed. O young Christian! enter at once into this confidential relation to the Lord. Ask him for teaching, ask him for holiness. Who was it that said to Paul: "My grace is sufficient for thee?" It was "the Lord," it was Jesus. For, hear the apostle's boast: "Most gladly, therefore, will I rather glory in my infirmities, that the power of Christ may rest upon me."[114]

Adorable Jesus! I am dark with sin; I am laden with iniquity. Be thou my light and my salvation. Teach me truth; teach me duty. For thine am I forever. Amen.

ENTIRE CONSECRATION.

Father, Son, and Holy Ghost,
One in Three, and Three in One,
As by the celestial host,
Let thy will on earth be done;
Praise by all to thee be given.
Glorious Lord of earth and heaven.

Vilest of the sinful race,
Lo! I answer to thy call:
Meanest vessel of thy grace,
Grace divinely free for all; Lo!
I come to do thy will,
All thy counsel to fulfill.

If so poor a worm as I
May to thy great glory live,
All my actions sanctify.
All my words and thoughts receive:
Claim me for thy service, claim
All I have, and all I am.

Take my soul and body's powers;
Take my mem'ry, mind, and will;
All my goods, and all my hours;
All I know, and all I feel,
All I think, or speak, or do;
Take my heart, but make it new.

MY BROTHER.

All men, of all ages, climes, and complexions, have a common parentage; all are involved in a common fall; all are regarded by a common salvation. Wherever he comes within the range of our help, every human creature is entitled to our beneficence. It is the law of the Old Testament and of the New. Second only to the love of God, is the love of man. The true maxim of philanthropy is: Thou shalt love thy neighbor as thyself The Spirit of Grace awakens and perpetuates this disposition in every subject of renewal.

But while the Law of Love enjoins this temper of helpful kindness towards all the children of Adam, it nowhere commands a chimerical and impracticable regard for all alike. It has no levelling philosophy, to equalize affection for all objects, and thus diffuse emotions so thinly as to reduce them to an inefficient indifference. The Gospel recognizes *degrees* in the outgoings of the heart. It owns the names of husband and wife, parent and child, brother and sister, friend and neighbor, coeval and countryman. It lays on us the duty — rather it confers the privilege, of loving some more than others, and brethren in Christ more than all. And as if for a guide and permission in all ages, even among the apostles there was one disciple whom Jesus loved, preeminently, and with a singular glow of melting affection. So that the way is prepared for us to consider yet more nearly the lesson of the Scriptures.

1. In our little analysis of this Christian love, it may be well to begin with one of the lowest, and therefore most intelligible principles of the attachment. We find that affection springs up among those who have *intercourse, association, and community of thoughts and interests.* The inquiry becomes abstruse if we push it too far into recondite sources; but the fact is open to all the world. You have — unless you are the most forlorn of men — a friend. You carry him often in your willing thoughts; you crave his presence, and are drawn toward him by an irresistible fascination; you are complacent when he is near you, even in silence and inaction; you sigh when long separated; you plan what shall give him pleasure; you reproach yourself when be is pained. In the degree of your regard, you are willing to labor, to dare, to suffer for his sake. You take fire when he is calumniated; you are happy when he is praised. But I will not rehearse the manifold operations of friendship. Whence came all this? As has been admitted, some of the springs are remote and obscure; but some of them are fully in view. There has been some companionship. Without this there may be respect, admiration, even distant love; but oh! how different from the fervors which kindle after delightful society, and the long commerce of heart with heart! This indeed would scarcely exist for so long a time, unless there were some congeniality of views and tempers, some opportunities of interview, some community of pursuit and aim. But day by day the band of wreathed attachments acquires new strands, till the fondness of youth becomes the sober but inviolable friendship of old age. Now all this finds its place in the association of Christian minds. Not, however, in the same degree, and therefore the amount even of religious love must vary. In a certain humbler sense, I may love the whole Church, as the unknown follower of Christ in Russia or Hindostan; but not as I love the companion of prayers and tears and

sacraments. The companionship of Christian service, devotion, daily life tends directly to the increase of this peculiar tie. And hence the most important practical rule — that if we would love the brotherhood we must cultivate Christian society. There is such a thing as a too insulated experience. That disciple must be crippled in his growth, who knows nothing of spiritual communion. We are not to make our pilgrimage as solitaries, nor to live out our days as hermits. Evangelical piety is eminently social. The constitution of the Church and all the means of grace evince this. What are our Sabbath assemblies, our social meetings for devotion, our common prayers, our mingled songs of praise, above all our sacramental communions, but so many ministries of holy fellowship? Despise them not; neglect them not; nor yet those more frequent and more informal interviews of friend with friend, in which the Christian character acts itself out, in the confidential flow of unstudied converse and tender reciprocal affection. If we have unfortunately allowed our emotions to be pent up, and our religion to become recluse and hidden, let us own the fault, and endeavor to flow together with at least one kindred mind, which seeks and prizes the same great objects with ourselves.

2. The principle is much the same, though operating in a higher plane, where we perceive, further, that Christian brotherhood is promoted by *a common object of affection*. Disciples agree in loving the Lord Jesus Christ, and this increases their love to one another. We see the effect of this cause, in common life. Attachment to the same friend or superior, knits hearts together. There are cases, indeed, where the result seems to be opposite, and where pursuit of the same object engenders rivalship, jealousy, and hate. It will be readily observed, however, that these are cases where the object is limited, and where only one can have

possession. Not so with the great centre of the believer's hope. As millions may bask in the vivifying rays of the natural sun, so all believers, without collision or envy, may look towards the same infinite God and Saviour. Thus it is in many a domestic instance. Who can doubt that the mutual affection of children is cemented by regard for the same parents? On the other hand, where unnatural divisions arise between one parent and the other, the little commonwealth falls into factions, or draws asunder in cold dislike. Soldiers of the same favorite commander, subjects of the same beloved sovereign, are by this very community of aim drawn into one. It were strange if this should not hold good in religion; where all adore and serve the same God, and all unite in devotion to the same Lord and Redeemer. Every disciple is a lover of the Lord Jesus Christ. The affection is characteristic and influential. Pervading great numbers with a common glow, it can not but fuse them together. They must grow in likeness. As crowds that press towards some one central object thereby are compacted together, so Christians come nearer to one another by coming nearer to Christ. That congeniality, which is inseparable from all friendship, is secured by the tender and awakened contemplation of the "one Mediator between God and man, the man Christ Jesus," especially when holy love, heightened by the sympathy of multitudes, gazes on his dying compassion, and gathers around the sacrifice of the Cross. Then it is, that "our fellowship is with the Father, and with his Son Jesus Christ."

3. Love of the brethren is promoted by the consideration that *all the brethren are objects of Christ's love*. I am naturally predisposed to love him whom my friend loves. All Christians are children of God, through Jesus Christ; and hence their relation is that of *fraternity*. The more we value the mercy and grace of the Redeemer, the more

shall we cherish those who are its objects. Ascertain that any human creature belongs to Christ, and you have made him near to you; though he were an Indian barbarian, whose language you could not comprehend. Therefore we can not love God and Christ without loving the brotherhood. Hence the apostle who reposed on Jesus' breast, makes it a test of sincerity. "He that saith he is in the light, and hateth his brother, is in darkness, even until now." "Whosoever loveth not is not of God, neither he that loveth not his brother." "He that loveth not his brother abideth in death." And, referring it to the very principle of the text, he adds: "For he that loveth not his brother, whom he hath seen, how shall he love God, whom he hath not seen?" It ought forever to drive away our selfish indifference toward fellow-Christians, that there is not one of them whom the blessed Lord has not loved even unto death. Can any paltry reason of self-interest be pleaded, in comparison with such a claim as this? Whatever the poor, contemned creature may be in earthly respects,. . *Christ loves him*, . . . that should be enough. But this cause becomes greatly more operative, when numerous believers consciously join at the same moment in acts of homage and affection, towards the Chief among ten thousand. Then, when all eyes have one direction, when all pulses swell with one sacred passion, when all voices flow together in concordant utterance of one name, when all tears combine to celebrate one feast of sacrifice, the sense of brotherhood is stronger than any where on earth. And this is the true glory of church-assemblies. For this the panting disciple longs to be gathered with the great congregation; to meet his *Lord*, and to meet his *brethren*. Even the neglected, unknown, and depressed servant of Christ, feels at such a time that his solitude is broken by the fellowship of adoring saints, and believes anew in the unity of the Lord's body. From which we learn how much brotherly love is cultivated by a diligent, hopeful and ardent attendance on acts of common worship, first in the sabbath assembly, and then in the more select and fraternal associations of piety. Either way then, by our love to Christ, by Christ's love to us, we are made to grow together in the bond of perfectness.

4. *The brotherhood all hear the resemblance of the Lord Jesus,* and therefore are dear to one another. The principle is thus stated by the apostle John: "Every one that loveth him that begat, loveth him also that is begotten of him." The love of Christ is essentially the same with the love of infinite moral perfection, or the beauty of holiness of which he is the highest impersonation. Every true believer is joined to Christ, receives his Spirit, and has the beginnings of a spiritual resemblance, which shall go on to perfect assimilation, according to the measure of each. The new nature craves this holy beauty, and loves it wherever descried. This is the chief source of Christian attachment. It is the affection for Christ, as mirrored in his members. "We hang with interest over the miniature of one who is beloved; and we value the living portrait of Jesus, even faintly drawn on the tablet of a fellow-saint. Christian love is determined to be such, when the attraction is something spiritual, and not any thing adventitious and earthly. The statement is simple, and can not now be dwelt on, but it is matter for reflection, and might penetrate the conscience, and reveal us to ourselves. It is obvious that, on this ground, a general increase of piety throughout the Church, or any part of it, will directly tend to the growth of mutual affection. That which is most for a lamentation is, that we bear so little of Christ's image, as to hold out scarcely any thing on which the strong regard of brother Christians can fasten. And this affords another motive for growth in grace. Yet we must not, on this account, excuse ourselves from the great social duty of our profession, nor

indulge a censorious turn for detecting blemishes in our neighbor, as a reason for our own churlish apathy. Let it suffice that Christ receives a brother; let us beware how we reject him. None will affirm that all holiness has vanished from the Church; and wherever it is, even in the slightest degrees, and with the greatest admixture, it ought to be amiable in our eyes. We should search for it, cherish it, and admire it. He who is inhabited by the Spirit can not be an object of indifference to the spiritual man. It is beautifully related of Origen, a great Christian author among the Greeks, that while he was yet an infant, his father used sometimes to approach his cradle, and uncovering his little bosom, would kiss it, saying, "Here is a temple of the Holy Grhost!" Somewhat similar should be our reverence for the work of God in every human soul. We should feel a profound awe in regard to that secret energy which goes forward in all saints. And wherever we discover the slightest lineament of our beloved Lord, we should be attracted, and won over. O that the day were come, when each of us might see in every other the infallible marks of that new life, "which after God is created in righteousness and true holiness!"

5. The love of brethren is peculiarly becoming to *those who expect to share the blessings of the future world.* In the way of similitude or parable, we might represent to ourselves a company of persons fighting their passage through an enemy's country to their beloved home. Could any thing be more natural than that they should cling to one another? The Christians of the present state are to be gathered in one glorious community, in that which is coming. Unless we have persuaded ourselves of the eventual salvation of all mankind, we know that from all but true Christians, there must be a final separation. Those who shall be our companions forever, may reasonably engage our affections

now. On this point, as on all that respects the future glory, there is a sad skepticism among the professed followers of Christ. If we had more lively apprehensions of that state towards which we are tending, we should conform ourselves to it in affection and life. The brotherhood of Christ's people would so grow in our estimation, that we should never become weary of cultivating their friendship, and enjoying their society.

SING PRAISES!

How joyfully does David cry, "Sing praises to God, sing praises; sing praises unto our King, sing praises; for God is the King of all the earth, sing ye praises with understanding."[115] Be exhorted, beloved brethren in Christ, during this season of gracious revival, to employ God's appointed method of psalmody, for setting forth the glory of his name, power and love. It may be a question whether, in the reception of such gifts, our silence has not been guilty.

I. SING PRAISES. Praise does not add to God's glory, but it glorifies him. "He that offereth praise, glorifieth me," saith the Lord of Hosts. To show forth the honor of his majesty and his love in Jesus Christ, is the chief burden of Christian song.

II. Sing to God and Christ. The two are not separate. Behold God in Christ; praise God through Christ. The soul looks out in this particular direction in praise. It is God and not man, who is generally addressed. Pliny writes to Trajan, that early Christians used to "to sing hymns to Christ, as God."

III. SING OF GRACE AND GLORY. You have noble themes, and enough to carry you up in song. The Church in all ages has had thc samc, and has celebrated them; but every new display of condescending love, and every new effusion of the Spirit, should lift and gather more sublime praises. If you have been converted, if your friends have been converted, then sing of grace and power.

IV. SING IN THE GREAT CONGREGATION. The swell of a

thousand voices is magnificent; and where they utter the high praises of God with the heart and soul, it is "the beauty of holiness." Even short of this, it is delightful, elevating, and edifying, to join with many voices. Let not yours be silent. The great meetings for prayer and praise, during this revival, are tending to restore to the churches the joint and mighty praises of congregational psalmody. "Let every thing that hath breath praise the Lord!"

V. SING IN THE MEETING OF BRETHREN. Whether the gathering be small or great, "sing ye praises." Why not have meetings for praise, as well as meetings for prayer? The Hebrew Church sang; the Temple worshippers sang, *the Lord Jesus sang.*[116]

VI. Sing in the Social Group. Young Christians should begin to learn this method of helping one another and honoring Christ. In the days of our ignorance how often have we prostituted our voices to worldly songs; and have we no praises at the fireside for our Redeemer? HENRY MARTYN was noted for this way of doing good. "He had an uncommonly fine voice, and fine ear;" says Mrs. Sherwood, who knew him in India; "he could sing many fine chants, and a vast variety of hymns and psalms. He would insist upon it that I should sing with him, and he taught me many tunes, all of which were afterwards brought into requisition; and, when fatigued himself, would make me sit by his couch and practise these hymns." If any think of RICHARD BAXTER as stern, let them read these words of his: "It was not the least comfort that I had in the converse of my late dear wife, that our first exercise in the morning, and the last in bed at night, was a psalm of praise, till the hearing of others interrupted it. Let those who savor not melody leave others to their different appetites, and be content to be so far strangers to their delights."

VII. SING IN FAMILY WORSHIP. Take time for it. Rob

yourself of ten minutes' slumber, or of ten morsels of food, but rob not God of his praise. The family is the school of praise, as well as of prayer and doctrine.

VIII. SING IN PRIVATE DEVOTION. Why not? The voice comes back with effect upon the heart. Solitude has witnessed your utterance of love-songs, comic-songs, idle, foolish songs; why should you not sing forth your love to Jesus? The whole book of Psalms may be profitably chanted in the closet, even by one who boasts no musical culture.

IX. SING WHEN THE SOUL IS JOYFUL. Psalmody is the appointed channel for the outlet and utterance of joy. "Is any merry," says the Apostle James, "let him sing psalms." When young converts meet together, they are sometimes liable to fall into light and unprofitable talk; nothing is better suited to pre vent this, and otherwise edify their souls, than to unite in spiritual and fervent hymns.

X. SING AMIDST THE REVIVAL OF RELIGION. "There is a time to mourn and a time to dance," that is, to rejoice in God. When should the children of the bridechamber rejoice, if not when the Bridegroom is with them? Now it is, that we go "to the house of God, with the voice of joy and praise, with the multitude that keep holy day." It is the joy of harvest. There is joy in heaven, over repentant sinners; let there be joy on earth; and let it have its rightful expression in high praises. The lofty anthem of united hearts and humbly exultant churches should now glorify our redeeming God, with the swell of harmony.

XI. SING WITH INTELLIGENCE OF THE TRUTH. "God is the King; sing ye praises with understanding," cries David; which Paul re-echoes thus: "I will sing with the Spirit, I will sing with the understanding also." Psalmody includes instruction. To reject all hymns which are didactic, were to reject some of the noblest inspired hymns. Thirteen psalms have for their title MASCHIL, that is, "didactic." The

Divine Word flows from mind to mind in fraternal instruction by means of psalmody. "Let the word of Christ dwell in you richly in all wisdom; *teaching and admonishing one another* in psalms and hymns and spiritual songs, singing with grace in your hearts to the Lord."[117]

XII. SING WITH ALL THE HEART. Empty indeed are all songs and praises which do not carry up the affections. The words which holy hymns suggest to us do often, by the influences of the Holy Spirit, produce or awaken the very graces which they express. But this is more especially done by the influence of melody and harmony, and the electric current to and from numerous worshippers. Yet only the adorable Spirit of God can preserve us from taking mere natural elation for that "joy of the Lord" which is our "strength!"[118]

XIII. SING IN THE CHURCH BELOW, so that you may sing in the Church above. When we think of heaven, it is with the idea of perfect adoration, love, and praise. This glorious outgoing of soul expresses itself best in song. There, in the world of perfection, "they sing the song of Moses, the servant of God, and the song of the Lamb, saying, Great and marvellous are thy works, Lord God Almighty; just and true are thy ways, thou King of saints." The ascriptions of rapt souls, throughout the Apocalypse, take the form of musical utterance. Those vocal acclamations of palm-bearing and harp-bearing saints must be regarded as psalms, songs, hymns, or anthems. Thus must we judge of the Four, and the Four-and-twenty.[119] They sing a "new song," saying, "Thou art worthy," "for thou wast slain!" The subsequent voice of the "ten thousand times ten thousand, and thousands of thousands," is the voice of song. The angels, and elders, and four living ones, who fall before the throne on their faces, and worship God, can not but utter the voice of celestial psalmody when they say: "Amen, Blessing and glory, and wisdom, and thanksgiving, and honor, and power, and might, be unto God forever and ever. Amen."

The nearest approach which we can make on earth to the joy of worship in heaven, is when we unite in hymning God and the Lamb. Oh! let us seek to engage in this service with heart and soul, as feeling that our powers have no more honorable and exalted use, than when we devote them to the praise of the Almighty Redeemer. This, we believe, is sometimes felt in a humble measure, during those delightful melting seasons, when at sacraments, or the concourse of thousands to hear the Word, or, as has recently been the case, in prayer-meetings of unexampled size, the hearts of believers experience the mysterious ardors of love, and rise in joy, swelling with high praises, for the gift of Jesus, and the conversion of multitudes of souls. May God grant us nearer and nearer likeness in our worship to the song of the redeemed!

REV. 5:6.

Behold the glories of the Lamb,
Amidst his Father's throne,
Prepare new honors for his name,
And songs before unknown.

Let elders worship at his feet,
The Church adore around,
"With vials full of odors sweet.
And harps of sweeter sound.

Those are the prayers of all the saints.
And these the hymns they raise;
Jesus is kind to our complaints,
He loves to hear our praise.

Eternal Father, who shall look
Into thy secret will?
Who but the Son shall take that book,
And open every seal?

He shall fulfill thy great decrees;
The Son deserves it well:
Lo! in his hand the sovereign keys
Of heaven, and death, and hell!

Now to the Lamb that once was slain,
Be endless blessings paid:
Salvation, glory, joy, remain
Forever on thy head.

Thou hast redeemed our souls with blood,
Hast set the prisoners free,
Hast made us kings and priests to God,
And we shall reign with thee!

The works of nature and of grace
Are put beneath thy power,
Then shorten these delaying days,
And bring the promised hour.

THE HARVEST OF NEW-YORK

There are some evils which belong to all great cities as such. The vastness of population brings ignorance and irreligion into greater proximity, and so to speak, congests them within narrow compass. Hence we find poverty, sickness, sloth, intemperance, mendicity, and fraud, on a larger scale, and with less surprise, than in other localities. Depravity is the same, indeed, "in the void waste or in the city full;" but in a metropolis sin is more crowded and more overt. The love of money, which is a root of all evil, operates more actively where so much wealth is in perpetual, large, and rapid circulation. Cupidity, fraud, and violence exist wherever man is found; but in cities they have a wider field, and come up to our notice every day of our lives. This familiarity with evil clearly tends to its propagation. It is just as true of vice as of contagious disease. The forced and unnatural nearness of man to man, renders it more easy for evil principles and practices to diffuse themselves, by precept and example. Crime and its provocatives are kept in countenance by the number and consequent boldness of transgressors. The same density of human actors renders easy every sort of associated action and combination. Idleness and luxury and love of pleasure are evil every where; but who does not know how violent a stimulus they receive in cities? For example, the wealth and voluptuousness of the great are continually working downwards, and corrupting the humbler classes. No man needs to go in search of means of intemperance; the invitation is at every corner. Few are the great towns in which the example of Sabbath desecration is not held out, almost ostentatiously, thus producing its like in the careless and the young. The public amusements of cities are not rare and occasional; their flames are kept up, night after night, as a perpetual sacrifice. Their invitations are blazoned on every wall, and that is a happy parent who can keep his children from coveting the forbidden gratification, almost before they have left the nursery. The *streets* may be called an ever-open school of vice; and there are hundreds of errant children of both sexes, whose whole education may be said to be that of the kennel. It is in cities that we naturally go to look for the extremes of pauperism, filth, and domestic misery; for cellars and garrets unventilated, unwashed, and overstocked with human inmates; for lofty buildings, swarming at each new flight with improvident, noisy, unhealthy creatures. Nowhere but in cities does the phenomenon occur, of scores, hundreds, thousands, and tens of thousands, who seem to be totally unrecognized out of their narrow circle, who live as they list, and who sink with every successive year into a more malignant corruption. In London, for example, the recent labors of Mr. Mayhew have revealed what may be called an underground population, numbering its hundreds of thousands, of whom multitudes know no marriage-tie; and of whom the great majority attend no place of worship. There would seem to be a *nation* growing up in the heart of Christendom, within daily sound of its church-bells, utterly destitute of the first rudiments of Christian instruction. And of these a large number, already mature and inveterate in evil, find their way to our shores, and to our very thresholds.

It is truly wonderful how many comfortable and well-doing persons live and die with scarcely any knowledge of these things. They sit in their drawing-rooms, or roll in their coaches, with scarcely a thought of the masses of ignorance, misery, and vice, which are almost touching them. Amidst purple, fine linen, and daily sumptuous fare, we forget the Lazarus at our gate, who is chiefly recognized by the dogs that lick his sores. These things are in all populous cities, but men of comfort see it not, or see it with vacant and abstracted gaze. To learn the details of this frightful reality, citizens must begin to observe and enumerate the squalid creatures that cross their path; must diverge into shaded and obstructed streets and alleys; must follow the mendicant and the chiffonnier to his attic or his hovel, and comprehend the nights of those who lurk about our thoroughfares by day. There is not a great city in Christendom, in which it is not true, that a large proportion of these classes is absolutely uncared for, in regard to true religion. And it adds to our alarm, that we need not go so far down in the scale of society, to find hundreds who are heathenish in their repudiation of all Christian observances, on Sabbaths or other days. All that has thus been said of cities in general, applies with full force to the city of our abode; while there are other considerations, somewhat peculiar to ourselves, which point us out as beyond question a ripe and suffering harvest-field.

It is to be expected that the largest city of the Western world should hold forth prominently those characteristics on which we have touched. Its very greatness just so far multiplies the occasions for religious endeavor. We begin to talk again and truly of the spring and buoyancy of our trade, the expansion of our commerce, the rise of property, the accumulations of capital, the magnificence of dwellings and equipage. These things should make us humble and thankful. But what if these blessings should be accompanied with increase of sins and famine of the word of God? Wealth breeds luxury, pride, and forgetfulness of the things of eternity. I was just now speaking of the poor; but here are causes which operate upon the rich, and in some cases upon ourselves. Read what the prophecies say of great cities in the old world; of Tyre, of Sidon, and of Damascus. In a very observable degree, the unparalleled growth of our city has tended to moral and religious decay, by change of residence and rapid fluctuation of people. We appear to live in a perpetual tide, which sweeps away in its course not only the mansions of former times, but the very sanctuaries where our fathers worshipped. Justifiable, nay, inevitable, as these mutations may be, they can not be accomplished without leaving large spaces more or less destitute of the means of grace. And already the whole southern portion of our Island presents a spiritual desolation, which affects the hearts of God's people, and in regard to which every one of us has a responsibility and an obligation. It is not enough that we secure the means of grace for ourselves and our happy children, who could obtain them even if suddenly left unsupplied; what is to become of the myriads who care for none of these things? Shall we say to them, from out these established houses of worship, "Go, serve other gods"? Many of our churches present the appearance in a great measure of repositories for sheaves already garnered; while on every side of us the fields are covered with luxuriant crops, which no husbandman is cutting down.

The influx of strangers from remote regions, and of emigrants from abroad, is giving a peculiar character to our city population. Of these, the great majority are without evangelical religious means. I am persuaded that very few among us are awake to the transformation which is passing upon us, from this single cause. The living cargoes, which are poured in upon us day by day, from Ireland and the European continent, and of which the worst dregs and sediment are arrested just here, and abide among us, are increasingly making their influence felt, on our manners, our morals, our religion, our elections, our municipal government, our police and prisons, our hospitals and our bills of mortality. We are in the midst of a gradual and silent, but tremendous revolutionary movement. Of Gremans alone, the accession has been such, that you may walk through whole streets, if not wards, in which their type and signature stand out with all the colors of transatlantic towns. Romish churches, convents, and schools are rising with incalculable rapidity. A nation of people owning spiritual, if not temporal allegiance to a sovereign beyond the seas, is consolidating itself in the midst of us. Not to assault or abridge their religious rights do I say this, but to indicate the greatness of the home-field, which calls for our zealous exertions. But we are not sure that this is the worst part of the foreign immigration. Protestantism has lost its glory in the land of Luther. Those subtle but dreadful forms of infidelity, which were broached by philosophers in their closets and professors in their chairs, became popularized, and worked their way downward through the strata of society, until they at length became intelligible to the lowest minds, and popular among the turbulent rabble. As in the French Revolution, so in Germany, these doctrines of the "Friends of Light" connected themselves with a passion for liberty, and with reformatory agitation. Ever since the outbreak of 1848, the convulsed masses have been heaving with equal violence against the altar and the throne. In any great movement towards emigration, it is obvious that none will be so ready to forsake their country, as those who after such sentiments have been disappointed. Many of the ringleaders in these commotions have reappeared in our land.

Turning to the indigenous population, with which we are more familiar, we find untold multitudes of the laborious as well as the unthrifty classes, who never enter a place of worship. "We find a juvenile throng, growing up without the knowledge of morality and salvation. We find large tracts of closely settled people, wholly unsupplied with the means of grace. And here I may let the curtain fall; for we have observed enough to demonstrate, that in whatsoever direction we turn our eyes, the fields are white already to harvest.

My beloved fellow-Christians, the theme is too grave, and the affair too urgent, for me to use any circuit in arriving at the practical conclusion. We must do something, and that without delay, or these evils will increase beyond our power of control. "The King's business requireth haste." While we slumber the enemy is coming in with fearful strides. And what are we doing, in our staid, respectable, and wealthy churches? What breakwater are we erecting against such a flood? Are we meeting the demands of our responsibility, of our very safety, by maintaining the proper and decorous service of God in our several sanctuaries? No man will pretend it. Vast harvests require extraordinary and immediate labor. But where is it put forth among us? At what point, or on what day have the united Christians of New York arisen in their strength, jealous for the Lord of hosts, and determined to carry the torch of light into these dark places? "Where is the concerted effort of evangelical laymen, to set up Gospel means in the deserted lower wards of this city? This harvest will not come in of itself, but must perish on the open field. To meet this exigency is our appropriate business as Christian churches. Life is short; and when after a few years some wanderer shall pick out our names, upon the marbles of a cemetery, what traces shall we have left behind us of our zeal for Christ and souls? It is for such efforts, and such self-denials, and such sacrifices, that God has bestowed on us our talents, our influence, and our means. Let me take it for granted without argument that the Christian Church was not founded solely for itself, and for promoting its own spiritual comfort and advantage; and further, that every particular church is called upon to diffuse blessings around its limited circle. This is especially true of churches which, have outlived the precarious and struggling period of existence. There is a stage in church-life, when every effort is needed to fill up its vacancies, sustain its service, and secure its continuance. But when this is past, and providence smiles upon its temporalities, assuredly it has arrived at the crisis of outward activity. The genius of Christianity is not simply that of conservation, but of aggression. It must not merely live, but increase and cover the earth. It is not an outpost garrison, fixed and stationary in its defenses; but an army, burning for conquest and going on by rapid marches and increasing victories. And this has been most signally manifest in every age of Church history, in which believers have evinced the true life of the body. Equally true is this of particular churches. They must break forth in action and increase, or they must dwindle and die. And let me affirm it with emotion, when any religious society has reached the point in which its complement has been made up, its forces organized, its seats filled, and when accordingly it can not longer hold forth wide invitations to the multitudes to come in, the conjuncture is solemn, I had almost said alarming. Nor is it matter of doubtful speculation, what a church in such circumstances should do. It should break out on the right hand and on the left. It should enter into the Lord's harvest. It should go out into the highways and hedges, and compel men to come in. It should have compassion on the ignorant and the outcast, who surround it. It should provide the means of grace for those who are destitute. There is work enough to be done, and there are means to do it.

Let me add with profound satisfaction, experience has shown in New York, that so far as the contribution of worldly means is concerned, there has never been any backwardness. But there is a want of enlightened zeal, as to the special mark of evangelizing the suffering population amidst which we dwell. And there is a want of concert and cooperative endeavor, in the right application of instruments. The case is this: the harvest is ripe, but the laborers are few. The Gospel must be preached by more voices among the ignorant and needy. They will not supply this want themselves, but will infallibly go from bad to worse. Here our intervention is needed. The church must be carried to those who will not come to the church. It never was the intention of Christ, that his word should be sustained among people of competency alone. Where Christianity is vital, the poor have the Gospel preached unto them. A wise and vigilant survey must descry the points in our great city, from which as centres the assault may best be made on the forces of unrighteousness and error. The message of life must at such points be proclaimed at once; *freely* at first, until men shall have learnt the necessity, the economy, and the delight of sustaining the church for themselves and their children. One such station, well manned, will become the *point d'appui* for successful operations all around. The best nucleus for a church is often the Sunday-school. It naturally connects itself first with smaller meetings, and then with the services of the Sabbath. It may be new to many, that in carrying out this simple and effective plan, the greatest difficulties sometimes insuperable have arisen from the want of a *place* in which to gather the uninstructed youth. Scholars teem, in our overcrowded tenements, by hundreds and thousands. Teachers, upon due summons, are not found altogether wanting. The purse of religious beneficence has been found constantly open to every well-judged summons. And yet our schools have been known to knock in vain at the doors of every sufficiently capacious public edifice. Now, I desire my readers to show cause, why it would not be a proper outlay of our ample means, for liberal Christians to secure ground before it is too late, and erect substantial and fitting edifices, with ample apartments for Sunday-schools. These might be occupied, during the week, by good schools, in which the Bible and religious doctrines should be taught. They would resound with the voice of prayer and praise, in social meetings, to which the surrounding poor would be invited. They would imperceptibly grow into places of Sabbath-service, where the Gospel should be preached to the perishing. In process of time they would be organized, and perhaps self-sustaining. But this is only one of many means which might be employed. That *some* means should be speedily used, is as clear as day. Let us pray to the Lord of the harvest, that he would thrust forth laborers into his harvest. But while we pray, let us not forget to labor ourselves. The times are favorable for Gospel effort. The mighty mass is as yet unformed and ductile. Souls are perishing every hour. The evil is not in India or Africa, but at our doors. And our time of action is very soon to have an end.

COMPEL THEM TO COME IN

The worst and vilest may be saved. Mighty awakenings do not stop short of the leprous and abandoned sinner. "When the Master of the house was angry, because all his invited guests began to make excuse, and refused to come to the Great Supper, though all things were ready, he thus gave orders to his servant: "Go out quickly into the streets and lanes of the city, and bring in hither the poor, and the maimed, and the halt, and the blind." As this was not enough, he gave a second order: "Go out into the highways and hedges, and compel them to come in, that my house may be filled."[120] "Who are these but the extremest outcast sinners? Such abound in our city, and perish for want of Christ.

There is in grace a wonderful power of growth, which, under God, is our hope in regard to society. It is salt, it is leaven, it is seed, it is light; these are Scriptural figures, all importing diffusion. In revivals of religion we observe this very remarkably exemplified. From one individual, we see the spark kindling upon a whole family, and from one family, reaching a church or neighborhood. But what we desire to witness, and what we should pray for, is, that Christianity in its vital power should reach far and deeply into the worst layers of society. O brethren! what must become of these self-destroying masses, unless they receive the truth!

When the Lord Jesus was engaged in his ministry on earth, he did not limit his regards to those who call themselves the better classes. "The common people heard him gladly." Remark was often made upon his tolerance of the wicked: "This man receiveth sinners and eateth with them." He was a "friend of publicans and sinners." Of the multitudes who went out after him, thousands were doubtless poor, and thousands were blind and vicious. Sons of affliction and daughters of infamy heard his gracious words. People of this sort have not only sense of misery but consciousness of guilt. They are often stung and lashed by remorse. In a sort of desperation they sometimes cry to God. They are frequently more ready to be impressed by the glad tidings than church-going formalists. Jesus spake to their hearts, and his gospel is still suited to such. In the great awakenings under WESLEY and WHITEFIELD, there was nothing more, remarkable than the degree in which the Gospel was carried home with power to the souls of the very lowest. "My rule," said John Wesley, "is to go not only to those who need me, but to those who need me most." The wretchedness which drove people to Christ was not altogether spiritual in the first instance, though in the Divine providence it had spiritual consequences. He who came for loaves and fishes found the bread of life; she who brought her vessel to the well of Sychar, received living water. So now, the sullen anguish of poverty, discontent, and disease, in cellars, garrets, and over-crowded and pestilential tenements, engenders longings which only the Gospel can gratify. Alas! alas! how slender are the means as yet employed for carrying the Gospel to these extreme points! Yet to these very points the Gospel may be carried with the best hopes of success. It were a dangerous error to presume that the inmates even of the odious resorts, noted and watched by the police, are necessarily devoid of thoughts about religion, and gnawing though vague consciousness of sin. Could we unroof dense portions of this great city, and look into the dens of drink, and play, and debauchery, we should behold the undeniable signs of wounded spirits, without hope, without God. The Gospel is made for such, and has saved such. Amidst the reiterated and increasing prayers which go up for the outpouring of the Spirit, surely there ought to be importunate supplication for influences to penetrate these lowest strata. Awakening is incomplete unless it go deeper, far deeper down, than our well-dressed throngs. Blessed be God, that these have the privilege; but oh! we crave it for the abject and abandoned. Nor will the victorious progress be complete till it reach the felon, the drunkard, and the 'strange woman.' In regard to these dangerous and desperate classes, a voice seems to issue from the holy place: "Whom shall we send, and who will go for us?"

Although places of instruction and worship are greatly needed for the miserable and vicious, and although all wealthy Christians should feel guilty until such be established, it is not enough to provide these means. Experience proves that good houses may remain empty, and able preachers unheard. We need a shock, to rouse these benumbed souls; an impulse, to urge them toward inquiry; a mighty drawing, to bring them to the Word. Their chief want is that of interest, awakening, motive; something to make them go to church, and care for their own souls. Popular reformations, under the truth, have this effect in some measure. Indeed we can think of nothing more likely to compel the attention of base, violent, and blasphemous men and women, than a mighty tide of revival, pressing its repeated waves into their miserable homes and hearts. Bad influences are propagated thus, why not good influences? All through the electric circle of a certain class, one hour will suffice to thrill the morbid passionate excitement of a prize-fight, a murder, or a rising mob; why should not the same human conductors bear such, impulses as have driven multitudes to hear a Luther, a Whitefield, or a Spurgeon? Would to God that we could see the day in which the messages of salvation and the meeting for prayer should be crowded by the very class who now fill drinking-shops, dance-houses, caverns of lawless pleasure, and jails! Nothing will effect this but great unexampled awakening; and for this we are to pray. If we carefully read what our blessed Lord spake in parable concerning the two sons, we shall see that these are the people who not only need the truth, but who are accessible to its power. "Jesus saith unto them, Verily I say unto you. That the publicans and harlots go into the kingdom of God before you."[121]

When in so remarkable a manner God is displaying his readiness to convert great numbers to himself, all who fear his name and love the souls of men, ought to be prostrate before him, in beseeching cries, that he would vouchsafe to urge the work of grace more widely and profoundly through the depraved multitude. As certainly as faith and love beget prayer, so certainly will prayer beget action; and means will be used to evangelize the lowest and vilest. Means are already attempted, but they will be better sustained. The blind and vicious, from whose ranks the levies are made for riots and prisons, will not flock to the preached Word, until some fresh and irresistible influence, affecting the whole population, find its way to the very scenes of their nocturnal orgies. Prayer for such an influence is clearly laid before us as a duty. While we pray we must work. These children of the wicked one will not come to the light; it must be carried to them. By territorial division; by canton of labor not too large to be manageable; by turning on a force of godly men and women large enough to visit with frequency; by making the effort in concert and exhaustively, so as to leave no nook or corner untouched; and by giving to the miserable some tidings of that rich gospel feast which awaits their acceptance, we shall instrumentally "compel them to come in." Unbelief as to the power and willingness of God to do this, is at the bottom of all our neglect and wrong action in this matter. If for a moment we fancy such an event as the conversion of our degraded and dangerous classes, the incredulous principle replies: "Behold, if the Lord would make windows in heaven, might this thing be?"[122] An awakening which should shake the dry bones in all the lowest populations, rousing them from filth and drunkenness, and raising up an exceeding great army to fight the good fight of faith, is more than we dare ask of God. And yet, brethren, it is not more than we may reasonably expect on Scriptural grounds, nor more than the eyes of the Church shall joyfully see, in the day when, by the Spirit, she shall rise to the height of faith and entreaty. Such a glory will be like that in respect to which the Lord comforts Zion in prediction: "Light up thine eyes round about, and behold: all these gather themselves together and come to thee. As I live, saith the Lord; thou shalt surely clothe thee with them all, as with an ornament, and bind them on thee, as a bride doth."[123]

THE PENITENT'S HYMN TO CHRIST.

My Saviour, canst thou welcome back
  A wanderer gone so far astray —
Whose heart ten thousand terrors rack,
  Ten thousand sins to wrath betray?

Fain would I come, fain would I fly
  To lay my burden at thy feet;
And in abasement ever lie
  Tearful before thy mercy-seat.

But feebleness and guilt and shame
  Restrain me, and I sink oppressed:
There is no favor I can claim.
  No place in Jesus' spotless breast.

Thus do I tremble, yet once more
   My flowing eye looks up and sees
The griefs thy sacred body bore,
   Thy scars, and blood, and agonies.

"Ah! not for me, these pains were borne!"
   Such is the guilty spirit's cry:
"Ah! not for me!" the soul forlorn
   Reiterates with many a sigh.

For thee! lost sinner, yes, for thee!
   Such answer from that marred face:
For thee, though sunken in guilt's sea,
   This sacrifice hath purchased grace.

All crimsoned over with thy sin,
   Welcome, lost sinner, welcome now;
These arms were spread to take thee in,
   This head for thee in death did bow

Melted by love, by pity won, I yield me.
   Saviour, to thy love,
The streams that from thy heart have run
   Shall every spot of guilt remove.

HELP THE SEAMAN

We read, "And the sea gave up the dead which were in it."

I. *Consider the* NUMBER *of the dead who are in the sea.* Both the small and the great are there. From remote ages it has been the receptacle of mortal bodies. Reflect on the whole generation which sank like lead in the mighty waters, when the fountains of the great deep were broken up, and the floodgates of heaven were opened, and all the high hills that were under the whole heaven were covered; and every living substance was destroyed which was upon the face of the ground. These millions shall yet be given up. The early navigation of the renewed earth did but fill the devouring chasm of seas and oceans. If the commerce of that day was less adventurous and large, it was more full of peril. "Without our compass or our science, the daring sailors of olden time threw away their lives more lavishly. The Roman poet had reason to exclaim at the temerity of him who first trusted himself to a perishable plank. The ships of Tarshish went down by thousands. The early Phoenician navigators added hosts of corpses to the ocean cemetery.

The Mediterranean, or Great Sea, was the chief field of ancient seamanship, and its waters were an ever-gaping sepulcher. Age after age beheld a large portion of mankind consigned to these depths. Dreadful as it is to be suffocated in the tempestuous waves, no single mode of death has had so many triumphs. To this must be added the vast fleets of warring nations, which were dashed together in battles, and driven asunder by storms; as in the conflict between Xerxes and the Greeks, in which hundreds of vessels were destroyed. But it is to modern navigation and commerce that the destructive element has looked for its most numerous victims. The seamen of the world of Christian nations are reckoned at more than two millions. The perils of human life are made the subject of accurate calculation; and those who are familiar with life-annuities know that, while ship-masters are allowed to insure at a double rate, common seamen are not allowed to insure at all. This significant fact affords a glimpse of the fatality which is attributed to the calling. Some have believed that the majority of sea-faring men die upon the waters. Scarcely a day passes without its loss; and our shipping-lists are records of disaster. It is not merely by dozens, or by scores, but sometimes by hundreds, that the remains are swallowed up; as when some lordly Indiaman goes down in the mid ocean. Perhaps this moment witnesses, amidst darkness and tumult, the cry of expiring agony. Thus, year after year, and century after century, the ocean has been receiving its tribute of corpses by thousands and by millions, until the great basins of the earth have become the receptacles of a large portion of those who have lived. The consideration of their number then should awaken our interest in those who go down to the sea in ships; for each of the dead has an immortal destiny, and every such soul cries to us to be in earnest, in expectation of that day when the sea shall give up the dead which are in it. It will give them up, in overwhelming magnitude of array, at the inevitable summons.

II. *Consider the* MANNER OF DEATH *which befalls those who are in the sea.*

Those corpses, ancient or recent, floating or at rest,

whole or dismembered, and even dissolved to atoms, are now motionless. But they each went down with a separate gasp and struggle. Each wrestled with the gigantic element; each cried out in the impotent shriek for help. It is not to appall the imagination that this harrowing picture is presented. It is to call on you for Christian provision against such a death. Benevolence labors, in Gospel lands, to prepare men for the awful hour of departure, even though hoping it may take place in the arms of friends, upon beds of ease, perhaps with lingering succession of warnings. And shall we have no kind forecast for the hour when the mariner is summoned, all at once, to his cold death-struggle? For here is death in a form which demands great grace for its support. Against such terrors, there should be the provision of unusual faith and trust. No principles of religion can be too strong for a shock so tremendous. The call is usually sudden. It is alarming. It comes amidst confusion, uproar, hurried exertion, desperate struggles for safety. If a multitude suffer together their faces do but reflect blackness on each other, and society here affords no solace. Who has not read of the frenzy of such an hour, or (horrible to relate) of the rush of dying men, in the mania of hopelessness, to the spirit-room? If on the other hand, the solitary wretch, exhausted and no longer clinging to his plank, clenches his powerless hands and sinks into his dark, cold, lonely depths, he needs not less the inward breathing of hope in Christ, when far from every voice, of mother, sister, or pastor, that ever whispered to him of salvation. Who in such a juncture can hope that the careless and it may be profligate one shall be able to gather his broken thoughts sufficiently to regard the object of faith? It is too late in such a moment of horror to collect the fragments of a neglected or forgotten creed. We speak often of the doubtfulness of such repentance as occurs on a *death-bed;* but what shall we say of a departure in the paroxysms of the strangling tempestuous sea! The fear, the delirium, the pain, of this crisis may even obliterate every thought of mercy. Let me then, by all the dreadful pangs that hover over the manner of this death, beseech you to lose no time in seeking to prepare for heaven him who may be thus summoned. For how unspeakably glorious the privilege of him, who, howsoever sudden his last alarm, can serenely, even when all human hope is gone, fold his arms, and raise his dying eyes, and from amidst the very gulf exclaim: "I know whom I have believed— death! where is thy sting? O Sea! where is thy victory?" Among converted seamen there have been many such. Their number, we trust, is daily increasing, by means of Christian exertions. Such we doubt not are in our port. Nay, such may be among the readers of this page. And it is to provide against a trial so common, and yet so fearful, that our efforts should be directed. For when the sea shall give up its dead, the difference will be marked, between those who have been driven away in their wickedness, by the storm that wrecked their hopes, and those who have had hope in their death; even though that death was in the surges of seeming destruction. Let the manner of this death, conjoined with its innumerable subjects, call you to new exertions for the soul of the mariner.

III. *Consider the* CHARACTER *of those who become the dead of the sea.*

If these were all men of God, neither their number nor their mode of departure would demand our intense sympathy. However the silver cord might be loosed, or the golden bowl be broken, they would have emerged in spirit from the waters of death into the joy of their Lord. But we have painful reason to believe that they are, in a vast proportion, unacquainted with these hopes: and "the ungodly are not so, but are like the chaff which the wind driveth away." Let us praise God that there are delightful exceptions of mariners who have learned the grace of the Gospel; who have praised the Redeemer and prayed to him amidst the storms of every sea; men whose voices have joined in the praises of God's people; and who have rallied under the most blessed of all flags, on which they have loved to read, in the language common to all saints, BETHEL, "the house of God." But these are the very persons who will most readily acknowledge, in all sadness, that the majority of their brethren are of a different stamp. The character of the seaman is more marked than that of most other classes, because the influences which go to form it are more exclusive, constant, and uninterrupted. The very disposition which leads the youthful mind to seek the adventures of the sea is not unfrequently one of hazardous excitability. And no sooner has he bid adieu to his native land, than he falls under the concentrated influence of causes which, in ninety-nine out a hundred instances, mould the nature. *Absence from home,* for such long periods, and during the better part of life, is a potent agency. The sea has no firesides; no quiet evenings; no domestic charms; no smile of the sister, the daughter, the mother; none of the humanizing influence of the gentler sex. Man is a foe to man when these kindly agencies are wanting. I do not believe it possible for a great number of our sex to be thrown together for long periods, whether in a convent, a prison, or a ship, without some moral hardening. Seamen may be said to receive all the formative influences from one another; and this at a distance from all the varied methods of instruction which, even unobserved, are perpetually operating at home. And then, who can estimate the power of this single peculiarity in their situation — that *they have no Sabbath!* When the ten thousands of Israel are going up, one day in seven, to appear before God, in the beauty of holiness, the mariner on the waste ocean, even though he be a disciple, lacks all memorial of holy time. With the greater part this sacred day has dropped out of the calendar. To measure the operation of this single cause, it would be necessary to consider all the unspeakable blessings of the Lord's day, the solemn worship, the ministry, and the sacraments. In the absence of that which is good, the human heart without grace preys on itself. Devotion needs these stated props and aids; hence divine wisdom and love has appointed them. Even private intercourse with heaven is apt to be forgotten, in the total absence of public means: which, indeed, is one of the great arguments in favor of the efforts for which I now plead. But seamen are not left in this innocent neutrality. They influence one another, and that sometimes after a fearful sort. The young sailor sometimes finds himself, on his earliest voyage, admitted to a school of vice, with adepts and veterans for his instructors. And when he sets foot on a foreign shore, after the labors, and perhaps disasters, of a voyage — after the weariness and disgust consequent on his exposure and duress —it is no wonder that he runs riot in his brief liberty, and yields to the extreme seductions of foreign ports. We have but to open our eyes and ears to know the mode of life adopted by sailors in our port after return from long voyages. The avails of long labor are sometimes squandered in a night. The wolves that raven for them are on the watch, prowling for the moral prey. Hence drunkenness, gambling, revelling, and debauchery. How often do these outbreaks call for the municipal force! How often does the wronged and deluded wretch cry for justice on his destroyers! How often are our ears rent by the unusual and heaven-daring profaneness of the throng of mariners! In many foreign ports all the influences are disastrous. There is every bait to vice, while there are no aids to virtue. The sharper and the seducer are there, but no preacher of righteousness, no flag of gospel-peace. Hence it is by no means wonderful, that, with the exceptions which we delight to admit, the character of seamen, as a class, is not such as to give us comfort in the expectation of the day when the sea shall give up the dead which are in it. Multitudes have gone down to that death with all their sins upon their heads. Having lived contrary to God, and brutalized themselves by passionate indulgence, they have sunk without hope. And oh! is there not a reason here why we should be using renewed exertions to cover the dangerous seas with Christian seamen?

IV. Consider the neglect with which the dead that are in the sea have been allowed to go down into its depths. *Neglect* of individuals or classes is to be measured with some reference to their importance and value. Were the seamen who are daily perishing in the waters an idle, unprofitable, burdensome generation, we might perhaps let them drop away with less blame. But they sustain the trade of the world. Whatsoever is meant by that pregnant word, *Commerce,* involves the toils and dangers of thousands of mariners. To neglect them is to cast from us the very instrument by which the gains of merchandise are acquired. The useful products, and the almost necessary luxuries, which are exchanged between continents and islands, are borne on their arms. The sails that fan all climates are guided by their sinews. There is not a delicacy or an ornament of commerce, there is not a wonder of art, there is not a transmarine medicine, there is not a transportation of Christian mercy, nor a visit of holy friendship and affection, which is not in some sort intrusted to the hardy seaman whom we neglect. And when he *dies,* far from sight of land, he dies in the hard service of a civilization and refinement which use him, and abandon him. The *soldiers* of the earth are many; but we can do without them. The day, we trust, is hastening on, which shall render obsolete their trade of blood. But the *sailor* we can not do without. The more peace, the more commerce. The progress of every science and art tends to bring a greater throng into this highway of nations. And the Gospel itself, as it begins to expand itself more largely over the earth, will claim for itself a Christianized seamanship, to disperse the word and the ministry of God among all nations. Mariners are then indispensable; yet these are they whom we have neglected. The sin lies at the door of Christendom. The son who leaves the maternal threshold to traverse the earth, is the one who should be famished with means of life. But the Church has seen her children going abroad over all waters, and yet has done but little, and even that little but lately, for the spiritual good of the seaman. How long was it before Christian watchmen even *missed* the sailor from church-assemblies? How long before means were used to furnish his sea-chest with the Bible? How long before a Bethel-flag was hoisted, or a Bethel-chapel built? While we bless God for what has been done, and for the encouragement we have to proceed, we can not but bewail the absolute destitution of the vast body of mariners. Immense portions of the Christian world take no cognizance of them as immortal beings. Congregations send up prayers, for years, without remembering those whose business is in the great waters. And the consequence is, that, although no field of effort has yielded more fruit in proportion to labor bestowed, yet so vast is the amount to be compassed, that the great mass is not reached. Neglected mortals continue to plunge unprepared into eternity. It would be a consolation to the pallid, shivering seaman, as he spends his few last moments on the parting timbers, before the final plunge, to remember some word of promise — some hour of communion — some message from Christ's ministers — some precious sacrament — alas! what multitudes have none such to remember! They have come and gone for years to and from Christian ports, but they have found no Christian privilege there; for none has taken them by the hand, or led them to the house of prayer. A poignant sense of this neglect moved the founders of Bethel Societies to begin and prosecute their work. They were willing to snatch, if possible, from the double destruction of soul and body in shipwreck, at least here and there one among the thousands who mount up to the heaven and go down again to the depths, while their soul is melted because of trouble; all this being but the beginning of sorrows. Neglect of such will appear in its true light when the sea shall give up the dead which are in it.

V. Consider our MEETING IN JUDGMENT with the dead who are in the sea. That hour is coming, and we should draw from it motives for our daily conduct. There are things which *may* or may *not* befall us in the future; but we must all stand before the judgment-seat of Christ. What a day of revelation will that be of all our neglects and transgressions! and how little, in the retrospect, will many of those things seem, which now occupy all our thoughts and passions! There is One coming who will say to some: "Inasmuch as ye did it not unto one of the least of these my brethren, ye did it not to me." The hour hastens. Behold He cometh, and every eye shall see Him! Hear the beloved disciple: "And I saw a great white throne, and Him that sat on it, (the shadowy vagueness of the representation only makes the approaching cloudy tribunal more fearfully sublime,) and *Him that sat on it,* (no *name* is needed, for there is one object now for every eye; and one sound reverberates in every ear and through every cavern of earth and sea,) from whose face the earth and the heaven fled away; and there was found no place for them." This judgment-bar is awful, is real, is approaching, is for us — you and I shall be attracted by irresistible fascination to that burning centre, and form part of that countless assemblage. Sinner! sinner! prepare to meet thy God! "And I saw the dead, small and great, stand before God" — before God! before Him from whose presence heaven and earth just now fled. The dead, in all their races, are there; of all tribes and nations; of every age, a ghastly multitude whom no man can number. All graves and sepulchers release their prisoners, of all times and ranks, from Abel downwards, to stand before God. "And the books were opened; and another book was opened, which is the book of life: and the dead were judged out of those things which were written in the books, according to their works. *And the sea gave up the dead which were in it.*" Now is the time of revelation from the mighty waters. Here are the deposits of solitary disasters, of thousands of shipwrecks, of vast fleets, and this through centuries of years. The faithful sea shall give them up at the voice of the archangel and the trump of God. The voice that awoke Lazarus and the youth of Nain, and which unseals all sepulchers, shall find obedience in the seas. No matter what the variety of life or death, there shall be *one* rising again, to look upon the face of God. How gladly would some call on rocks and mountains to cover them; or seek a deeper plunge into the concealment of the ocean! but no —

"Seas cast the monsters forth to meet their doom,
And rocks but prison up for wrath to come."

YOUNG.

LORD, HEAR THE SEAMAN'S CRY!

Awaked from gentlest midnight sleep,
I hear the howling blast,
The chamber rocks, the murmur deep
Of ocean rises fast.
The lurid flash, the thunder's roar,
Proclaim the tempest nigh,
And wavering lights are off our shore —
Lord, hear the seaman's cry!

This hour, perhaps, the sailor thinks
Of wife or mother far.
As, drenched and spiritless, he shrinks
At some portentous bar.
The cresting foam betokens death.
The breaker's rage is nigh,
He prays— with quick, redoubled breath-
Lord, hear the seaman's cry!

Ah! many a youth now lost in sin,
And many a hoary sire,
Who never prayed, this night begin
To dread Almighty ire.
In headlong fury, while the bark
Pierces the billows high,
They learn to pray in anguish Hark!
—Lord, hear the seaman's cry!

Though sinking in the whelming flood
  In solitary woe.
Saviour, thy ever precious blood
  Can reach thy hapless foe.
Catch the faint, smothered voice of him
  Whose penitential sigh
Rises amid the terror grim;
  Lord, hear the seaman's cry!

Pray for the sailor, ye who rest
  Upon your curtained bed;
Pray to the Power at whose behest
  The fearful storm hath sped.
And when, released from fear and care,
  Sweet hours of night glide by,
Be sometimes this your fervent prayer,
  Lord, hear the seaman's cry!

J. W. A.

TO FIREMEN!

'HARK! One — two — three — four — five! Yes, it is our district! Here it goes — throw my cap after me — there is not a moment to be lost!' So cries the stout and gallant young American, as he dashes from his door at dead of night, while the street resounds with "Fire, fire, fire!" In less time than you have taken to read these lines, thousands have poured out, joined their respective machines, and choked with living masses the avenues leading to yonder column of black smoke and towering flame. There is scarcely on earth a scene of greater excitement. The valiant and youthful soul is stirred as the war-horse with the sound of the trumpet. Amidst the thick of the encounter, the din, heat, smoke, shock, and shouting, there is all the excitement of a battlefield without its blood, and all the peril of an assault without its wrath and malice. The true-hearted fireman, he who is urged on not by fame, or pride, or drink, but by honor, duty, and humanity, is a soldier of peace. His perils, darings, and achievements sometimes equal those of Waterloo or Lucknow; but he seeks to save not to *destroy* life.

Hence it is, that we honor the fireman, and look to him as the brave protector of our hearths and our children. When we contemplate a procession of these stout-hearted men and youth, careering through our streets on some gala day, with gay appointments and brilliant equipage, we seem to behold the muscle and sinew of our commonwealth, the defenders of our homes, the sons, and brothers, and husbands who would fly at a moment's warning to resist invasion or quell intestine violence; and we involuntarily exclaim, God forbid such hearts should be the prey of infidelity, drunkenness, or lust!

It is a noble sight to behold a well-built, stalwart, symmetric human form flushed with health and vigor. And it is melancholy to see such a figure rendered partially useless by the loss of an eye or an arm. But the beautiful balance and proportion of the bodily frame is not so much marred by the loss of an eye or an arm, as the inward man, the spiritual and immortal part, is disfigured by moral evil. For what can be more hideous and revolting than to hear words of lying or profaneness from lips of manly grace; to see a powerful arm prostituted to unlawful violence; or to witness the downfall of a fine, graceful form into the kennel of intoxication! Hear, O young man, hear the voice of a friend1 The counsel of the loving mother, sister, or wife, in such a case, is safest and wisest. Flee from the snares which would weaken and cripple your powers of manhood. You would scorn a man who should deny that *Honesty is the best policy;* but do you not yourself reject the equally undeniable truth, that *Holiness is the highest happiness?* Listen to the voice within; the voice of reason, of conscience, and of the Word; the voice of God calling you to true blessedness.

Why may not even a worldly man, as yet irreligious, be made to admit that there is a happiness in noble impulse? Why shall he not acknowledge that there is something more exquisitely pleasurable, than the dance, the play-house, the tavern, or the debauch? You know what we mean by noble impulses. See yonder, where the walls of that burning house are trembling towards their fall, while timber after timber plunges crackling and flaming into the steaming furnace within. Look, where, in that lofty corner, unreached as yet by the consuming element, a figure in white madly stretches forth imploring hands, and seems to shriek, though all voice is swallowed up in the clamors of the terrible hour. There!

after baffled attempts, the ladders are set and braced. A brave fellow, amidst showers and clouds of smoke, mounts, enters, seizes that fainting daughter, bears her on his shoulders, just in time to clear the sinking ruin that thunders with a crash, and among acclamations of sympathy and praise, gives the rescued maiden into a father's arms. Such events are the glory of the fire department; and for one who actually achieves such a distinction, there are a hundred who would attempt it or desire it. Now, who hesitates for a moment to pronounce the delight and transport of this generous and heroic young man to be immeasurably greater than that of a hundred gains, and a hundred frolics? This is what we mean by noble impulses. And it shows how much soul-pleasures, heart-pleasures, true manly pleasures, surpass the joys of the body and of sense. But there are other, and even higher impulses of the noble soul; AND THEY ARE TO BE FOUND IN RELIGION. Yes, that Christianity from which you have perhaps turned away as from a dull, sour, long-faced, wearisome thing, wakes up souls to these higher impulses and joys. If there are some who would rather seek money and amusement than go to church; so there are some who would rather sit at low revels, with beer and cards, than risk life and limb to save a fellow-creature. But your soul despises them; and you say: "Give me the nobler pleasure." Ay, say further: "Give me the *noblest!* Give me the love of a divine Saviour, and the love of my fellow-men for His sake!"

The other day a fireman, who fell at his post, was carried forth to burial. Sudden death is no unusual event in these ranks. But men who walk so near the flaming brink of danger should be prepared. Every stroke of the fire-bell, when it booms through the stillness of night, should syllable these words: PREPARE TO MEET THY GOD! Cast from you the unreasonable and unscriptural belief, that all men go straight to glory when they die. It was not the priests, but the blessed Jesus, meek, and lowly, and loving, who spake of the "unquenchable fire."[124] Take up your neglected Bible, and see if this is not so. Do not rush on blindly, in voluntary ignorance, but place yourself in the light. On this topic, as on others, respect the judgment of those who have given it most attention. Seize the first opportunity of going to the house of God, and keep up the habit. Compare what is there taught with what you read in the Bible. Try to find out whether there is not something real in the attractions which have urged into a religious life some of the purest, loveliest, and bravest of the human race. Brother fireman, do not be duped by men who say that religion is for women and cowards; but read a little about Col. Gardiner, and Hedley Vickars, and Henry Havelock. Can any of your scoffing friends live more bravely or die more happily? Oh! if you would have their prize, follow their footsteps.

You have, it may be, enjoyed the instructions of a pious mother. The memory of a mother comes with power over a brave man's heart; it is a manly tear which he sheds over her grave. Do you believe she was sincere? Then follow the path which her gentle wisdom long ago pointed out. Let her Saviour be your 'Saviour,' and her God your God. Dread an everlasting separation from her, and from all the holy, and from Jesus Christ, at the Day of Judgment.

Reader! Despise not this gentle pressure of a friendly hand. Receive the affectionate advice of these pages. You are a guilty and perishing sinner; and you know it. But Jesus Christ offers you pardon and salvation. Repent and believe the Gospel. Accept the message of one who had been before a blasphemer, and a persecutor, and injurious: "This is a faithful saying, and worthy of all acceptation, that Christ Jesus came into the world to save sinners; of whom I am chief."

THY FATHER SEES.

From the German of Ch. K. L. von Pfeil.

Thy Father sees! Be on thy guard:
Thy Father hears! Be still:
Thy Father conies, oh! stand prepared
To learn his holy will.

The Lord of Light thou canst not see,
Though day and night most near;
Keep thou his Word perpetually,
And say, "My God is here!"

Whatever word thou wouldst not say,
Whatever work wouldst shun,
If God were by thee, clear as day —
Leave thou unsaid, undone.

And if in danger or distress,
Thy youthful heart be brought,
Believe, with constant hopefulness.
That God forsakes thee not.

Know that whatever can displease,
And what thy joy has marred,
Each care and want and woe he sees
With fatherly regard.

To him in faith forever cleave,
As if thou saw'st him nigh;
In trust that he will never leave
The souls that to him fly.

Say to him, child, "My Master, see
  Us children, in distress;
To thee, Father, we our plea
  In life and death address."

1 AMPLE HISTORIES OF THE REVIVAL MAY BE EXPECTED FROM THE COMPETENT PENS OF THE REV. DR. PRIME AND THE REV. DR. CHAMBERS.
2 PSALM 104:30.
3 JUDGES 5:16
4 ACTS 2:13.
5 EXOD. 32:26.
6 MARK 3:22. LUKE 11:15.
7 ACTS 5:39.
8 LUKE 15:7.
9 ACTS 8:8.
10 JOHN 19:35.
11 2 COR. 5:17.
12 1 COR. 16:22.
13 JOHN 20:19, 26. ACTS 1:14; 2:1.
14 PSALM 122:6.
15 EXOD 17:10, 12.
16 EZEK. 36:37, 38.
17 MATT. 18:14.
18 ROM. 6:17.
19 HEB. 12:29.
20 ROM. 15:30.
21 ISA. 6:1-6.
22 2 TIM. 2:17
23 GAL. 1:24.
24 JAMES 5:20.
25 JAMES 5:20.
26 PSALM 66:16.
27 JOHN 1:43-51.
28 MARK 8:36.
29 1 COR. 9:19,22.
30 PHIL 3:18.
31 EPH. 2:12. 4 JONAH 1:6.
32 ECCLES. 9:10.
33 LUKE 13:9.
34 LUKE 20:20.
35 PROV. 14:32.
33 LUKE 13:9.
34 LUKE 20:20.
35 PROV. 14:32.
36 GEN. 4:9.
37 1 SAM. 26:19.
39 PSALM 142:4.
40 GEN. 2:23.
41 DAN. 12:3.
42 PSALM 81:10.
43 PSALM 102:13, 14.
44 LUKE 11:13.
45 MAL. 2:15.
46 JOHN 3:34.
47 LEV. 8:12.
48 PSALM 133:2.
49 1 JOHN 2:27.
50 EZE. 39:29.
51 JOEL 2:28.
52 PROV. 1:23
53 JOHN 16:7.
54 ACTS 2:33.
55 COMPARE ACTS 1:4, 5,14; 2:1.
56 ACTS 10:44; 11:15.
57 1 PETER 1:12.
58 ZECH. 4:6.
59 1 THESS. 1:5.
60 1 COR. 2:4.
61 JOHN 3:5,6,8.
62 TITUS 3:8.
63 JOHN 16:8.
64 ROM. 8:13.
65 1 COR. 6:11.
66 ROM. 5:5; 1 THESS. 1:6.
67 1COR. 12:6,7.
68 LUKE 12:12.
69 EPH. 6:19.
70 JUDE 20.
71 DEUT. 32:30.
72 NUM. 32:23.
73 2 COR. 6:2.
74 PSALM 95:8.
78 JOHN 5:28, 29.
79 GAL. 6:7.
80 ACTS 7: 51.
81 2 TIM. 2:26, MARGIN.
82 1 KINGS 20:11,12
83 MATT. 9:12.
84 COL. 3:3; ROM. 7:9.
85 PSALM 51:16,17.
86 ISA. 53; ACTS 9:27-39.
87 JOHN 1:29

88 LUKE 19:10.
89 1 TIM. 1:15.
90 ROM. 5:6.
91 GAL. 3:13.
92 1 PET. 1:19.
93 1 PET. 2:24.
94 ROM. 5:9.
95 GAL. 2:16, 21.
96 1 ROM. 3:24, 25, 26.
97 ROM. 5:1.
98 ROM. 8:1.
99 1 JOLM 2:1.
100 ROM. 5:19.
101 LUKE 15:2.
102 HEB. 6:18.
103 JOHN 13:13.
104 JOHN 20:16.
105 MATT. 11:29.
106 READ ISAIAH 59:21.
107 JOHN 16:13.
108 LUKE 6:46.
109 ROM. 3:20-28.
110 DEUT. 10:5.
111 COL. 3:24.
112 2 PET. 2:19.
113 1 JOHN 1:6.
114 2 COR. 12:9.
115 PSALM 47:6, 7.
116 MATT. 26:30.
117 COL. 3:16.
118 NEH. 8:10.
119 REV. 4:8-12; 5:8.
120 LUKE 14:23.
121 MATT. 21:28-32.
122 2 KINGS 7:2.
123 ISAIAH 49:18.
124 MATT. 3:12; MARK 9:43; LUKE 3:17.

CPSIA information can be obtained
at www.ICGtesting.com
Printed in the USA
FFOW03n1322230617
37078FF